RON E. M. CLOUZET

D0093952

DECODING
BIBLE PROPHECY

RON E. M. CLOUZET

DECODING
BIBLE PROPHECY

Pacific Press® Publishing Association
Nampa, Idaho
Oshawa, Ontario, Canada
www.pacificpress.com

Cover design by Gerald Lee Monks
Cover illustration by Nathan Greene
Inside design by Aaron Troia

Unless otherwise noted, all Scripture quotations are from The New King James Version, copyright © 1979, 1980, 1982, Thomas Nelson, Inc., Publishers.

Scriptures quoted from NASB are from *The New American Standard Bible®,* Copyright © 1960, 1962, 1963, 1968, 1971, 1972, 1973, 1975, 1977, 1995 by The Lockman Foundation. Used by permission.

Scripture quotations marked NIV are from the HOLY BIBLE, NEW INTERNATIONAL VERSION®. Copyright © 1973, 1978, 1984 by International Bible Society. Used by permission of Zondervan Publishing House. All rights reserved.

You can obtain additional copies of this book by calling toll-free 1-800-765-6955 or by visiting http://www.adventistbookcenter.com.

ISBN 13: 978-0-8163-2614-3
ISBN 10: 0-8163-2614-2

11 12 13 14 15 • 5 4 3 2 1

ACKNOWLEDGMENTS

This work was significantly helped by a group of readers, authors, and scholars who cared. What they did for this project has no price. Thanks go to Skip MacCarty, DMin; Marvin Moore, MA, MDiv; Peter van Bemmelen, ThD; and Herbert Douglass, ThD; for their careful, annotated, and expert feedback.

Thanks also go to Russell Burrill, DMin; Jack Blanco, ThD; Norman Gulley, PhD; Errol McLean, DMin; Ed Schmidt, DMin; Larry Lichtenwalter, PhD; and Shawn Boonstra; faithful friends who took important time to read the manuscript, or parts of it, and lent their valuable counsel. The book is better because of them. Any flaws in it, which surely exist, are my responsibility alone.

My gratefulness includes the fine people at Pacific Press®; Russell Holt, for his able editing; and Scott Cady, for facilitating the publishing of the book. And, of course, to my wife, Lisa, always my first reader.

To Lisa Lynn,
my loving wife and faithful ministry partner

CONTENTS

INTRODUCTION

"Judgment Day May 21."

Having captured my attention, the large billboard on NW Fourteenth Avenue in Orlando, Florida, went on to proclaim: "The Bible Guarantees It." You likely saw this billboard, too. There were twelve hundred of them scattered over America's highways and major intersections, plus another two thousand across the rest of the world. Tens of thousands of believers distributed literature in every major city and painted, "Save the Date! Return of Christ. May 21, 2011," on bus benches and even on their own cars, warning people of the day of reckoning.

In spite of many skeptics, Harold Camping, president and general manager of Family Radio, convinced hundreds of thousands that the looming Judgment Day of May 21 was exactly what the Bible predicts. But of course the day came and went without incident, and Camping set yet another date for doomsday.

The truth is that the Bible did not—and does not—proclaim the date for the end of the world, no matter how large the letters on the billboards. There is every reason to believe Harold Camping is a sincere and faithful Christian, but the conclusions of his Bible study—published on his Web site for all to see—leave much to be desired. He simply ignored basic rules of biblical interpretation.

You may wonder, *If godly people who make a habit of studying the Bible can miss it by a mile, what about the rest of us? How can we ever understand complex Bible prophecy?* The Pharisees during the time of Christ were professional Bible students, yet they missed the greatest event ever—the coming of their Messiah!

You need not despair. Jesus said that God's Word, the Bible, "is truth" (John 17:17), and that if we know the truth, the truth will make us free from the devil, who "does not stand in the truth" (John 8:44). Paul commended a young man by the name of Timothy for studying the Scriptures, which made him "complete, thoroughly equipped for every good work" (2 Timothy 3:17). If Timothy could be so successful studying the Bible, so can you.

Keep reading. Help is on the way. In this little book, you will learn basic, sound principles of Bible and prophetic interpretation that will help you avoid basic pitfalls when studying God's Word. You will learn the meaning of mysterious symbols and the key to deciphering major prophecies. You will get into some specific passages of Scripture and come out at the end, saying, "So that's what that's all about!"

Millions today misinterpret Bible prophecy, in part because they don't know how to study it or because they trust others who supposedly know more than they do. Hang in there! Bible prophecy was meant to be a great blessing, and Satan knows it. He will try his best to bring confusion instead of clarity.

Make no mistake, this is a small book, but is not light reading. We get right to it in each chapter. Some statements and Bible references deserve more development, but this is not the book for that. Don't worry about some things that may not be perfectly clear yet. Commend yourself to the guidance of the Holy Spirit as you read. Seek to know God's will and His ways. And if something still does not make sense, be patient. God will put you in contact with further help.

At the end of the first century, the angel of the Lord made a promise to John the revelator that we can still believe today: "Blessed is he who reads and those who hear the words of this prophecy, and keep those things which are written in it; for the time is near" (Revelation 1:3).

The blessing is promised. Let's begin without delay!

CHAPTER 1
PROPHECY: A MATTER OF LIFE OR DEATH

David Koresh claimed to have the gift of prophecy, the gift to understand God's messages and convey them to his followers. The leader of a religious cult known as the Branch Davidians, Koresh considered himself to be the spiritual descendant of the biblical King David. He developed the "House of David Doctrine," which meant fathering twenty-four children with different women, some only teenagers. These children, he said, would one day serve as ruling elders during the millennium after the return of Christ.

Acting on reports of illegal weapons and child molestation, federal authorities besieged Koresh's Mount Carmel compound near Waco, Texas, for fifty-one days, seeking to enter. The standoff ended on April 19, 1993, with the now-infamous conflagration at Waco that left seventy-six dead, including at least seventeen children—and David Koresh himself.

"I am the Lamb," Koresh proclaimed to his flock, asserting his status as messiah, and "you are Koreshians." Revelation was his favorite Bible book. He also saw himself in the ancient Persian king Cyrus who was God's instrument of deliverance for the children of Israel after their Babylonian captivity (see Isaiah 44:28–45:4). "My Father, my God who sits on the throne in heaven, has given me a book of seven seals. . . . If America could learn these seals, they would respect me. I'm the anointed one. . . . It's the fulfillment of prophecy," he would preach.

In 1995, two years to the day after David Koresh died, Timothy McVeigh bombed the Alfred P. Murrah Federal Building in Oklahoma City in retaliation for what he considered to be the government's abuse of power against Koresh's cult. One hundred sixty-eight persons died, and almost seven hundred were injured.[1]

The Koresh and McVeigh stories are extreme examples of what can happen when otherwise decent people misinterpret the nature and purpose of Bible prophecy. It becomes a matter of life or death. Surprisingly often, good and evil, truth and falsehood, are indistinguishable for us human beings. This is due to our sinful human nature. Light often appears dark, and the dark we take for light. "There is a way that seems right to a man," wrote wise Solomon, "but its end is the way of death" (Proverbs 14:12; 16:25).

The nature of the prophetic word

Knowing our problem, God, in His marvelous concern for our welfare, devised a way to make up for that difficulty. It's called *revelation*. He revealed Himself—His will and His truth—through numerous prophets through the centuries of time, so we could actually tell what is truth from what isn't. A relatively small, yet sufficient, portion of that revelation was written down. We call that written portion the "Bible" or "God's Word." Such *special* revelation is God's gift to us. Paying attention to it brings life. Ignoring it leaves us like sitting ducks for Satan's imps to blow us right out of the water.

"And so we have the prophetic word confirmed," wrote the apostle Peter, "which you do well to heed as a light that shines in a dark place, until the day dawns and the morning star rises in your hearts; knowing this first, that no prophecy of Scripture is of any private interpretation, for prophecy never came by the will of man, but holy men of God spoke as they were moved by the Holy Spirit" (2 Peter 1:19–21).

This statement is a mouthful, worthy of at least a brief analysis. Four concepts come to mind. First, Peter calls the Bible "the prophetic word." He does so simply because the Bible was written by prophets, that is, individuals who spoke for God. The Greek *prophetes* (prophet) means "foreteller." So, God's Word is a *prophetic* word. However, prophecies are not *only* statements that have to do with the future—*predictive* prophecy. There is also *prescriptive* prophecy, or present truth. In other words, the prophets in the Bible not only *foretold* things to come, but they also *forthtold* things; they proclaimed eternal truth. Most of what we find in the Bible is not predictive in nature, but prescriptive.[2] Either way, the important thing, says Peter, is "to heed" God's Word "as a light that shines in a dark place, until the day dawns" in our hearts.

This point is critical. If we ignore what God said through His prophets, we will continue to abide in "a dark place." Have you ever been temporarily blind? All you want is to come to the light. Every fiber in your being longs for light so you can see things around you as they really are. This is why God's prophets in the Old Testament were also known as "seers" (see 1 Samuel 9:9). Darkness distorts your perspective, stops your progress, and renders you vulnerable to falls and injuries. Light is life. God's Word is regenerative; it produces something in us that was otherwise dead. Note what God said in Isaiah 55:8–11:

> "For My thoughts are not your thoughts,
> Nor are your ways My ways," says the Lord.

"For as the heavens are higher than the earth,
So are My ways higher than your ways,
And My thoughts than your thoughts.
For as the rain comes down, and the snow from heaven,
And do not return there,
But water the earth,
And make it bring forth and bud,
That it may give seed to the sower
And bread to the eater,
So shall My word be that goes forth from My mouth;
It shall not return to Me void,
But it shall accomplish what I please,
And it shall prosper in the thing for which I sent it."

But now back to Peter's enlightening statement. Have you noticed he said we should pay attention to the word of prophecy "until the day dawns and the morning star rises in your hearts" (2 Peter 1:19)? What does that mean? Is that a mere reference to daylight following night? No. In the Bible, the "morning star" is a reference to Jesus Christ! "I, Jesus, have sent My angel to testify to you these things in the churches. I am . . . the Bright and Morning Star" (Revelation 22:16). So, the explicit objective of all Bible prophecy is for readers to discover Jesus in the text.

This is the clear objective of the book of Revelation from the very start. The book begins with the words: "The Revelation of Jesus Christ, which God gave Him to show to His servants" (Revelation 1:1). Most Bible readers understand that classical prophecy speaks directly to ethical and moral issues based on the fact that they have a relationship with God. What they don't often realize is that apocalyptic prophecy—prophecy dealing with the end times—also speaks to ethical issues in our lives. Whatever God says there is not only for our information, but especially for our transformation. And the reason is the tie with Jesus. As we study prophecy, Christ Himself becomes more clear to us, and we feel compelled to surrender to His loving and just will for our lives.

How God inspired His Word

Thirdly, Peter's statement informs us who really is behind this Word of God: holy men of God who spoke "as they were moved by the Holy Spirit" (2 Peter 1:21). The Bible is not a book written by holy men, such as certain documents that some religions see as sacred because they were written by men considered holy. Being "holy" is not enough to discern right from wrong. It doesn't mean perfection. Holy men are responsive to God, but they are still men. Peter declares, however, that the Bible was written by the Holy *Spirit,* that is, by God Himself, who inspired the holy men who walked humbly with Him.

There is an important implication to this point. Many people assume that because the Bible is God's Word it cannot reflect the frailties of the human instrumentalities He used to reveal it to us. But that is a misunderstanding of the inspiration process. The apostle Paul said that "all Scripture is given by inspiration of God . . . that the man [or woman] of God may be complete" (2 Timothy 3:16, 17). The Greek word translated as "inspiration" is *theopneustos,* which literally means "God-breathed." God the Holy Spirit *breathed* His words and thoughts to the prophet. The prophet, then, wrote them down in his own words.

Except for the Ten Commandments and those places in the Bible where we find a "thus says the Lord," God did not dictate words to the prophets, but inspired them with thoughts, fully engaging their minds in the communication process. The writers' unique personalities, language skills, and personal experiences were preserved in the process. The prophets were not holy word processors but holy *men,* subject to the weaknesses and failures of men. Take, for instance, the book of Revelation, a book of apocalyptic prophecy. Scholars agree that John's Revelation is written in a peculiar form of Hebraized Greek, due to his constant use of Old Testament imagery and phraseology. Some believe that his use of the *Koine* (common) Greek is not linguistically perfect because he first wrote the book in his Aramaic mother tongue.[3]

Another example where the individuality of the Bible writers is apparent is in the four Gospels—Matthew, Mark, Luke, and John. If God had dictated His words to the Gospel writers, all four would have used the same wording for each related incident. But the authors had different objectives in writing the story of Jesus.[4] It is the different wording and nuanced details in each Gospel that show how God worked through each prophet or apostle just as he was.

Perhaps an analogy will help us better understand. If two men are walking by a busy city street and witness a collision at the corner, when authorities ask them what they saw, they are likely to use different words and even emphasize different details in their reports. Both stories are true and complement one another, but they are not identical.

Regardless of human limitations, God's Word "is living and powerful, and sharper than any two-edged sword, piercing even to the division of soul and spirit, . . . and is a discerner of the thoughts and intents of the heart" (Hebrews 4:12). God's Word "is a lamp" to our feet "and a light" to our path (Psalm 119:105). It is quite categorically the infallible Word of God even if written in human language. The reason? Its authors were men "moved" by the Holy Spirit.

Misinterpreting prophecy

One last point from Peter's comprehensive statement is that "no prophecy of Scripture is of any *private* interpretation, for prophecy never came by the will of man" (2 Peter 1:20, 21; emphasis supplied). This is very important. The Bible is not to be interpreted any way we wish. Many Christians today read the Bible and say, "This is what it means to me." In other words, "It doesn't really matter what the Bible *says;* what matters is what it says *to me.*" This is a very dangerous attitude. If we are to accept the words of the prophets as God's messages to His people, our objective should be to find out what *God* is actually saying—not what we would like Him to say.

Theologians and Bible scholars have two nifty words for this concept. *Exegesis,* meaning "to guide," is the proper approach to Bible study. We, the students, place ourselves *under* the Word, to be guided by it. We let the Bible tell *us* its reality, and not the other way around. *Eisegesis,* on the other hand, means "to guide into." That is what many people, sometimes even scholars, do. They come to the Bible with a certain body of knowledge and presuppositions and impose these onto their reading of the text. *Eisegesis* is reading into the Scriptures what we think they should mean.

For example, in the well-known prophecy of seventy weeks of Daniel 9, we read, "And after the sixty-two weeks Messiah shall be cut off, but not for Himself; and the people of the prince who is to come shall destroy the city and the sanctuary. The end of it shall be with a flood, and till the end of the war desolations are determined" (verse 26). This is part of an important prophecy we'll be looking at later. For now, I'd like to focus on just one word—*prince.*

Most people assume this "prince" must be an evil individual, interpreting him as the antichrist of the end-time tribulation or as Antiochus IV Epiphanes, a Seleucid king of the second century B.C. They consider this "prince" to be evil because of what the text says "the people of the prince" will do—destroy the city and the sanctuary, resulting in desolations, and so on. It's true that King Antiochus did some things that desecrated the temple, but he never destroyed the city of Jerusalem, so he can't be the "prince" mentioned in this prophecy. More importantly, however, neither Antiochus nor any other evil individual can possibly be the "prince" mentioned in verse 26, for the simple reason that the previous verse—verse 25—has already identified who the prince is! In verse 25, the angel tells Daniel, "Know therefore and understand, that from the going forth of the command to restore and build Jerusalem, until Messiah the Prince, there shall be seven weeks and sixty-two weeks; the street shall be built again, and the wall, even in troublesome times."

Now, read that verse again. Do you see that the Bible itself identifies who this prince is? The prince is the Messiah! The fact that most English versions capitalize the word *prince* in verse 25 but not in verse 26 does not mean it's not the same person in both verses. The Hebrew language in which the book of Daniel was originally written has no upper- and lowercase letters, so capitalization is a relatively modern tool that appears in Bible translations, but it is not an inspired tool found in the original languages—whether Greek, Hebrew, or Aramaic.

Why, then, do people assume "the prince" in verse 26 is not Jesus and that it refers to some sort of evil prince or antichrist? Because they read into the text what they have heard somewhere, were taught in the past, or assume based on other factors. They make the Bible fit into their frame of reference instead of making their thoughts fit into what the Bible says. When we come to a difficult Bible passage, the best thing to do is simply to allow the Bible to speak. That is the first rule of prophetic interpretation, as we will see later.

You may have more questions about the prophecy of Daniel 9, but be patient; we'll get to it in the next chapter and later.

You see the point, don't you? *Mis*interpreting Scripture can be very dangerous to your *spiritual* health. It can lead you astray. It can make you think a Bible text that applies to Jesus really applies to satanic agencies—the complete opposite of the Bible's intent. Even full-time students of the Bible, such as the Pharisees during the time of Jesus, fell into this trap. They interpreted Jesus' miracles as coming from the devil instead of coming from God (see Matthew 12:22–28).

Need for a surrendered heart

The Pharisees so easily misinterpreted Jesus' actions and words. For example, when He told them, "Destroy this temple, and in three days I will raise it up" (John 2:19), they thought He was speaking of the literal temple in Jerusalem, rather than metaphorically referring to Himself as the "temple" (see verse 19–21). The reason they so easily misunderstood was because their hearts were not right with God. They did not surrender themselves to God's Word even though publically they revered it. They made a pretense of loving it, but in reality they used it for their political or personal purposes. Jesus condemned that attitude. He said to them, "Well did Isaiah prophesy of you hypocrites, as it is written, 'This people honors Me with their lips, but their heart is far from Me. And in vain they worship Me, teaching as doctrines the commandments of men.' . . . All too well you reject the commandment of God, that you may keep your tradition" (Mark 7:6–9).

What a profound statement, in the light of much of what happens in the name of religion today! Most misunderstandings about prophecy—or about the Bible in general—are due to religious tradition or to our own personal presuppositions. We just get used to thinking in a certain way or doing things a certain way, and become surrounded by others of like mind, all the while darkening counsel by our lack of understanding, as God accused Job of doing (see Job 38:2). In spite of a myriad of commentaries and endless books written on Bible subjects, confusion remains about what it really says.

A sound approach is to ask ourselves: "Am I really surrendered to God's Word or do I hold on to certain interpretations of Scripture because I've become identified with them?" Sometimes, we feel that if we were to change our minds about what the Bible says on this or that point, we would lose a bit of our identity in the process. This can happen to any of us. But it is only as we surrender ourselves to God's Word that the way is made clear to understand His will. Didn't Jesus, the Master Himself, say, "If anyone wills [is willing] to do His [God's] will, he shall know concerning the doctrine, whether it is from God" (John 7:17)? First, surrender your will to God, and then knowledge of God's doctrine will follow.

"For whatever things were written before were written for our learning, that we through the patience and comfort of the Scriptures might have hope" (Romans 15:4). In my travels all over America and the world, I have seen firsthand evidence of the power of God's Word when people actually come *at* the Word with a submissive spirit of learning, rather than coming *to* the Word with preconceived ideas. Those belonging to the latter group cannot see what is so obviously before their eyes. The Spanish adage applies, "There is no worse blind man than the one who refuses to see." But for those who come humbly before God's testimonies, what light floods their souls; what joys fill their hearts; what insights flood their minds about the true love and character of God! This is life abundant!

Prophecy and prosperity

A long time ago, Ahab, the wicked king of Israel who was married to Jezebel, invited Jehoshaphat, the king of Judah, to join him in war against Syria at Ramoth Gilead. Jehoshaphat feared God and suggested they should "inquire for the word of the LORD" before doing so. Accordingly, Ahab "gathered the prophets together, four hundred men, and said to them, 'Shall we go to war against Ramoth Gilead, or shall I refrain?' " (2 Chronicles 18:4, 5). These prophets, whose main objective was to please the king, said, "Go up, for God will deliver it into the king's hand" (verse 5).

Jehoshaphat, suspicious of such a glib endorsement, asked Ahab if, perhaps, there was still "a prophet of the LORD" from whom to inquire (verse 6). So, they brought Micaiah, but as they did so, Ahab's messenger told him, "Now listen. . . . Let your word be like the word of one of them [the four hundred prophets], and speak encouragement" (verse 12). But Micaiah considered faithfulness to God more important than agreeing with the king, so when he prophesied, he was true to God's message. He warned Ahab that God had predicted that going to war would bring about Ahab's death (see verse 19).

In spite of this prophecy, the kings joined forces and went to war against the king of Syria at Ramoth Gilead. Knowing God had said he'd perish there, Ahab put on a disguise so no enemy soldier would recognize he was the king of Israel and try to kill him (see verse 29). But someone shot a random arrow into the sky "and struck the king of Israel between the joints of his armor. . . . And about the time of sunset he died." (verses 33, 34). So much for trying to outsmart God!

Just two chapters later, we read that the Moabites, the Ammonites, and the Timmanites from Mount Seir joined forces— this time against Jehoshaphat, king of Judah. The king sought

God's counsel, saying, "Our eyes are upon You" (2 Chronicles 20:12). He recognized that God can see clearly, while we cannot. He recognized that he must depend on God. God sent Jahaziel to the king of Judah and all the people. In God's name, Jahaziel told them to go to war and that they would not need to fight this battle, "for the battle is not yours, but God's" (verse 15). Based on this prophetic word from the Lord, Jehoshaphat did something as historic as it was amazing. He sent a choir ahead of the soldiers to meet the enemy! And "when they began to sing and to praise, the LORD set ambushes against the people of Ammon, Moab, and Mount Seir, who had come against Judah; and they were defeated" (verse 22). The singing brought such confusion to these idolatrous nations that Ammon and Moab fought each other, including the inhabitants of Mount Seir, until they were destroyed (see verse 23).

The lesson? When Ahab refused to listen to God's prophecy, he died. But when Jehoshaphat listened to God's prophecy, even when it didn't make sense to fight three larger armies, he was victorious. The corollary of all this was immortalized in Jehoshaphat's admonition to the people of Judah: "Believe in the LORD your God, and you shall be established; believe His prophets, and you shall prosper" (verse 20).

It's equally true today. Paying attention to the word of God's prophets is a matter of life or death. The book of Revelation declares, "Blessed is he who reads and those who hear the words of this prophecy, and keep those things which are written in it; for the time is near" (Revelation 1:3).

Is the time near?

CHAPTER 2
THE ABOMINATION AND THE COMING SIGNS

It was the last time Jesus would visit the temple of Jerusalem. He said to the Jews, "Your house is left to you desolate" (Matthew 23:38). As He walked away, His disciples followed, but they weren't quite ready for His next statement: "Not one stone shall be left here upon another" (Matthew 24:2).

How could this possibly be? Six centuries before, when Babylonian armies besieged Jerusalem, burning the city and temple to the ground, the Jewish leaders had been certain God would not allow this to happen. But He did. It happened because divine protection for Israel was conditioned on the response of the covenant people to their God. Blessings would follow faithfulness, but unfaithfulness would bring about death and destruction (see Deuteronomy 28:1, 2, 7, 13–15, 25, 47–52).

Christ's disciples, as well as every Jew in Jerusalem, were convinced they were now finally on the right path, never again to lust after other gods. How could the temple be destroyed again?

Fascinated and full of curiosity, the disciples asked Jesus, "Tell us, when will these things be?" They could only imagine the destruction of their beloved temple to take place at the *eschaton*—a fancy word for "the end of all things." So, they asked a second question for clarification: "And what will be the sign of Your coming, and of the end of the age?" (verse 3).

Jesus' answer constitutes the key to all prophetic interpretation. Keep in mind the disciples' two questions: (1) destruction of the temple, and (2) the sign of Your coming. Jesus answered both together in His Olivet discourse, spoken from the Mount of Olives—recorded in Matthew 24, Mark 13, and Luke 21.

First warning

Before He answered the disciples' questions, Jesus gave them a warning: "Take heed that no one deceives you" (verse 4). Christ's answer to their two questions involved many fascinating facts, but nothing was as important to Him about the destruction of the temple and the time of the end as the desire that His followers not be fooled! He stressed it three different times (see verses 4, 11, 24)! Clearly, this to Him was the big issue, because "even the elect [chosen]" could be led astray (verse 24). And the deception would come through false christs, false prophets, and miraculous wonders.

Here is our first lesson. When it comes to the study of end-time prophecies, expect deception to abound. Jesus did. "See," He said, "I have told you beforehand" (verse 25).

Fear is perhaps the most common feeling shared by many sincere people who are wondering about the end time—or at least a nervous uncertainty. They fret about a coming world-ruling antichrist, about whether or not they'll be part of the rapture, about the Tribulation, or about how the fearsome plagues of Revelation will affect them. But Jesus spent more time telling the disciples how to *prepare* for the end than giving them details *about* the end (see Matthew 24:32–25:46). He is our loving Savior, and His concern is not so much with "times or seasons" (Acts 1:7) but with the state of our hearts.

His byword to us has always been: "Do not fear, little flock, for it is your Father's good pleasure to give you the kingdom" (Luke 12:32).

The destruction of the temple in A.D. 70

Jesus gave the disciples a specific *sign* for each of their concerns. The sign to know when the destruction of the temple was near would be seeing " 'the abomination of desolation' . . . standing in the holy place" (Matthew 24:15). Luke's account of Jesus' words clarifies the meaning of this "abomination of desolation." According to Luke, Jesus said, "But when you see Jerusalem surrounded by armies, then know that its desolation is near" (Luke 21:20). That means that the "abomination" had to do with armies besieging Jerusalem, causing "desolation." Did that actually happen?

Rome took over Judea in 63 B.C. The empire implemented a policy of *Pax Romana*—a Roman peace—with all the nations it conquered; most went along with it, paying taxes to Rome while securing peace from their conqueror. But from the start, many Jews resisted Rome. Within a hundred years, the "wars and rumors of wars" (Matthew 24:6) Jesus predicted had reached a fever pitch. The temple priests had stopped offering sacrifices and prayers on behalf of the Roman emperor (emperors were considered gods). Judea was the only conquered nation to do so. Since this was considered treason, in A.D. 66, Rome sent Cestius Gallus, the governor from nearby Syria, to teach the Jews a lesson in humility. Once Cestius arrived, however, Jewish guerilla groups killed more than five hundred Romans. Fearing they had awakened a monster, the remaining Roman soldiers took refuge behind the temple walls, knowing Cestius would want to avoid attacking such a magnificent edifice.

Mysteriously, in spite of being on the verge of success, the Roman leader withdrew with his army and left the city! The Jewish historian of the day, Josephus, said the sudden change of the situation caused "many distinguished Jews" to abandon the city "as swimmers desert a sinking ship."[1] Almost forty years before, Christ had urged His followers to do the same: "When you see the 'abomination of desolation' . . . then let those who are in Judea flee to the mountains" (verses 15, 16). That is exactly what Christians did. The historian Eusebius wrote in the fourth century: "The church at Jerusalem, having been commanded by a divine revelation . . . removed from the city and lived at a certain town beyond the Jordan called Pella."[2]

The Romans, however, had not forgotten Jerusalem. Emperor Nero called on General Vespasian, who, along with his son, Titus, and many legions, marched on Jerusalem, starting a siege in the spring of A.D. 70. Many in the city died of starvation and disease; some even resorted to cannibalism, eating their own babies. Christ had foreseen this tragedy also, saying, "Woe to those who are pregnant and to those who are nursing babies in those days!" (verse 19). In spite of this horror, the city fathers refused to surrender, believing God could never abandon His temple.

By the end of August, some Roman soldiers were fed up with Jewish stubbornness. A group of Jews had again taken refuge in the temple. And even though Titus did not want his soldiers to touch the temple, some of them set it on fire. The gold-plated wood of the temple walls and ceiling burned to the ground, sending the soldiers in a frenzy to scrape the gold from every nook and cranny, thus turning every stone "upon another" (verse 2) in order to reach it. Eventually, Titus razed the city and the temple complex to the ground.

And so Christ's prediction was fulfilled. But the sign of the destruction of Jerusalem and the temple had a more comprehensive meaning.

The abomination of desolation

Jesus had made reference to the prophet Daniel in connection with " 'the abomination of desolation' " (verse 15). Six hundred years earlier, Daniel had prophesied, "And the people of the prince who is to come shall destroy the city and the sanctuary. The end of it shall be with a flood, and till the end of the war desolations are determined. . . . And on the wing of abominations shall be one who makes desolate" (Daniel 9:26, 27). These verses are part of the seventy-week prophecy in reference to the destruction of Jerusalem.

In the Bible, the word *abomination* is sometimes used in reference to idol worship (see 2 Kings 23:13; Isaiah 44:19). The word *transgression* means "sin." So, these similar expressions all lead to one conclusion: the abomination of desolation is pagan worship taking over the worship of God and causing the desolation of God's city, temple, and people. The same is true in spiritual terms. Turning away from Christ leaves one desolate, helpless, and hopeless. That's why Jesus, when rejected by the Jews, said to them, "Your house [the temple] is left to you desolate" (Matthew 23:38).

When the Roman armies besieged Jerusalem, they carried standards in the place of flags; these standards were emblazoned with symbols of pagan deities. Soldiers today salute their flag, but Tertullian, the second-century writer, tells us that Roman soldiers *worshiped* their standards.[3] Once the Roman soldiers destroyed the temple in Jerusalem, they set up their standards in the temple court and sacrificed pigs to them! Daniel 8:13 applies the term "transgression of desolation" to the symbolic "little horn" power. Some commentators have interpreted this "little horn" power to be Antiochus IV Epiphanes, the Seleucid (Greek) king who caused abomination by desecrating the temple and created desolation by killing many Jews. But he did this in 164 B.C., nearly two hundred years *before* Jesus was even around to make the prophecy! Obviously, Antiochus IV Epiphanes cannot be the "little horn" power since Jesus' prophecy placed that power in the future.

The truth is that for quite some time after the era of the early church, and since the time of the Reformation, many Bible interpreters have identified the beast in Daniel 7 as imperial Rome and have seen the "little horn" rising out of it as religious Rome, its natural successor.

The sign of His coming

But Jesus also predicted a clear sign for His second coming, in answer to His disciples' query. He said, "Then the sign of the Son of Man will appear in heaven, and then all the tribes of the earth will mourn, and they will see the Son of Man coming on the clouds of heaven with power and great glory" (Matthew 24:30). Paul adds detail to what Jesus said about His coming. He declared, "For the Lord Himself will descend from heaven with a shout, with the voice of an archangel, and with the trumpet of God. And the dead in Christ will rise first. Then we who are alive and remain shall be caught up together with them in the clouds to meet the Lord in the air. And thus we shall always be with the Lord" (1 Thessalonians 4:16, 17).

The *sign* of Christ's coming is the fact that He *Himself* is coming! Now, the fact that Jesus felt it necessary to identify His personal return as the sign of the end is very significant in view of His warning against being deceived. Evidently, the deception He warned about, brought about by "false christs and false prophets," who will "show great signs and wonders to deceive, if possible, even the elect" (Matthew 24:24) has to do with His coming, but not with He *Himself* coming.

Paul said Jesus will meet us "in the air" (1 Thessalonians 4:17). Many assume Christ will return to set up His kingdom on earth, but He wanted to warn us that only *false* christs would be on the ground when He comes. The true Christ will meet us in the air. When Christ ascended to heaven in full view of His disciples, "two men stood by them in white apparel, who also said, 'Men of Galilee, why do you stand gazing up into heaven? This same Jesus, who was taken up from you into heaven, will so come in like manner as you saw Him go into heaven' " (Acts 1:10, 11). Again, the emphasis is clear: Jesus *Himself* will return and will do so like He ascended, in full view of His followers, from the sky, in the clouds.

This truth is much more important to understand today than it was a few generations ago. The reason is that today many sincere believers are convinced the coming of Christ will be secret, not visible to anyone, and that the church will be raptured to heaven while a seven-year tribulation follows on earth. How so many came to believe this idea of a secret rapture will be the subject of the next chapter. Revelation says, "Behold, He is coming with clouds, and *every eye* will see Him, even they who pierced Him" (Revelation 1:7; emphasis supplied).

To summarize so far: the disciples asked when the destruction of the temple would take place and what would be the sign of Christ's coming and the end of the world. Regarding the destruction of the temple, Jesus gave them a specific sign—the presence of pagan armies in the temple area, an abomination that would lead to its desolation. He also gave them a specific sign regarding His coming—the fact that He *Himself* would come in the clouds. The Bible says God "makes the clouds His chariot" and "His angels spirits" (Psalm 104:3, 4). So, evidently, Jesus comes on clouds of angels.

What about other signs and the Tribulation?

What about the other signs of Jesus' coming? What about the "wars and rumors of wars" (Matthew 24:6)? Christ clearly spoke about them, saying in the same verse, "See that you are not troubled . . . the end is not yet." And what about the "famines, pestilences, and earthquakes in various places"? Again, Jesus assured them that "all these are the beginning of sorrows" (verses 7, 8).

Christ did go on, in verse 9, to speak about the tribulation the early church would go through. But this tribulation was to occur before the destruction of Jerusalem since Jesus did not bring up the " 'abomination of desolation' " until verse 15. And it is only in verse 21 that He identifies a "great tribulation, such as has not been since the beginning of the world" which happens, obviously, after the destruction of Jerusalem in A.D. 70.

Apparently, all the famines, earthquakes, wars, and rumors of wars are signs of the *age* more than they are signs of the *end*. Natural disasters, national and international conflicts, persecutions, and tribulations have been with us for two millennia. They characterize the entire period between Jesus' first coming and His second coming. They are signs of coming, but not necessarily signs of nearness. Jesus called them "birth pangs" (verse 8; Mark 13:8).[4] But this designation does imply that frequency and intensity in the signs means we're getting closer to the main event, just like a birth gets closer with the frequency and intensity of the woman's contractions!

These signs are designed to encourage believers to keep watching, to gather courage that Christ knew what He was talking about, and to look forward to the end. After all, the object of prophecy is not to wow people with upcoming events that are strange and fascinating, but to give followers reasons to believe in God. "Now I tell you before it comes," Jesus said, "that when it does come to pass, you may believe that I am He" (John 13:19).

But there is more. A careful analysis of this prophetic chapter shows that Jesus may have alluded to three distinct time periods in history. The first one spans the time from His day until the destruction of Jerusalem in A.D. 70, almost forty years (see Matthew 24:4–20). The second time period is the time of this great tribulation, which, when compared with other writings by Daniel and Paul, spans centuries (see verses 21, 22). And the last one is what the Bible calls "the time of the end," leading to the last days just before the return of Christ in the clouds (see verses 23–31). When you add what Daniel said about the time of the end, you find three times of trouble, or tribulation, together with God intervening three times to deliver His people. The table below compares these three times of trouble.

Categories	First Century Matthew 24:4–20	The Middle Ages Matthew 24:21, 22	The Time of the End Matthew 24:23–31
Tribulation	Persecution of early believers by pagans and insiders (verses 9, 10).	"Great tribulation, such as has not been" (verse 21).	A severe "time of trouble" right before God's saints are delivered and resurrected (Daniel 12:1, 2). This will include the seven last plagues.

Abomination	Pagan Roman armies at temple court to destroy it.	Ecclesiastical Rome usurping Christ's priestly ministry via the "little horn" (Daniel 7:25).	All the world worshiping the beast (Revelation 13:3, 12).
God's Intervention	"Flee to the mountains" (verse 16).	Tribulation cut short for the "elect's sake" (verse 22).	Angels will gather the elect from all over at Second Coming (verse 31).

One thing is clear: according to Jesus, the church will go *through* the Tribulation and will not escape it. In fact, He ratified this concept just one day after His Olivet discourse: "In the world you will have tribulation; but be of good cheer, I have overcome the world" (John 16:33). It is in the midst of His people's time of trouble that God intervenes on their behalf. This is consistent with Israel's experience while the plagues were falling in Egypt. Israel's deliverance—the Exodus—was not before the first plague, but after the last one. They were in Egypt through all the tribulation. God protected His own during that time of death and destruction (see Exodus 9:6, 23–26; 12:12, 13).

This evidence places into doubt the idea that the church must be raptured in order to avoid the end-time Tribulation upon the world. The consistent picture in the Bible is one in which God stays by His own during times of trouble (see Matthew 28:20; Psalm 91:3–16).

The ultimate message of Bible prophecy

The conclusion to our brief study of Matthew 24—Jesus' prophetic chapter—is that He is the center of all prophecy. Bible prophecy is not about the crisis of the end as much as it is about Christ living in our hearts until the end. He is the Rescuer of the persecuted, the Victor over the enemy, and the reason why the end will come. His visible coming is the sign of the world's end and of His return.[5]

On the other hand, Christ gave His disciples a specific sign—the one forecasting the destruction of the temple in Jerusalem. This represents another side of the prophetic coin. The "abomination of desolation" embodies all that is against Christ and His people. This is the enemy. And end-time prophecies operate within the parameters offered by these opposite entities—Christ and Satan, the Lamb and the beast. The enemy appears in prophecies as an antichrist, in various forms throughout history, who, unable to defeat God Himself, seeks with all his might to maim and destroy those who faithfully follow God. In Daniel, he is revealed as the beast and the "little horn" power (see Daniel 7: 7, 8, 24–26; 8:9–14), and in Revelation as the red dragon who is "enraged" with the rest of the woman's (the church's) offspring, that is, Christ's remnant people of the end (see Revelation 12:17). This great conflict between Christ and Satan, between good and evil, is the front-and-center setting for all end-time prophecies. Christ is the Rescuer of His people; Satan the persecutor.

The message from Ezekiel, from Daniel, from Revelation, from 2 Thessalonians, from Matthew 24, and from any other prophetic portion of the Bible dealing with the end time is simple: Christ wins! This is the context of the book of Revelation, for example, where John the revelator, "in the tribulation and kingdom and patience of Jesus Christ, was on the island that is called Patmos for the word of God and for the testimony of Jesus Christ" (Revelation 1:9).

John, had become known as the disciple "whom Jesus loved" (John 20:2). He outlived all the other apostles, and was pastoring the church of Ephesus in his nineties, when Emperor Domitian began a campaign of persecution against Christians in A.D. 95. Sullen and deeply disliked, the emperor decided to be honored as a god and demanded worship of his image throughout the empire. John, refusing to do so, was sent to Rome to be killed in a caldron of boiling oil. Though "plunged" in it, Tertullian reports, he was "unhurt,"[6] much like the three friends of Daniel were preserved in spite of being thrown into a fiery furnace (see Daniel 3).

When God miraculously rescued His faithful servant, Domitian banished him to the penal colony on the island of Patmos. It was in the midst of these trials that John was given the visions he relates in Revelation. Only eighteen months later, a new emperor, Nerva, came to the throne and had John released. In the book of Revelation, John picked up where Jesus left off, focusing on His second coming. "Behold, He is coming with clouds, and every eye will see Him, even they who pierced Him" (Revelation 1:7).

He *is* coming! Christ wins! That's the message of end-time prophecies. Christ rescues His people! But along with that message there are important end-time warnings and critical lessons for end-time people to understand. God, as a loving Father, forewarns us about the perils of the road. Yet, somehow, many miss the mark by a wide margin when it comes to interpreting His prophecies correctly.

The story of how we got to this sad point is the subject of our next chapter.

CHAPTER 3
THE STORY OF A WRONG APPROACH

It took eighteen hundred years before some of the prophecies found in the book of Daniel began to make sense. Yet, that too was prophesied. God had told His faithful servant, now well in his eighties, "But you, Daniel, shut up the words, and seal the book until the time of the end; many shall run to and fro, and knowledge shall increase" (Daniel 12:4). The "time of the end" would become almost a technical expression in Daniel, referring to the time after the fulfillment of the last time prophecy—the 2,300-day prophecy of Daniel 8. Since a prophetic day in the Bible means a literal year (see Ezekiel 4:6; Numbers 14:34), we've been living in "the time of the end" for almost two hundred years now.[1] In the early 1800s, knowledge of the book of Daniel increased greatly, causing people in America, Europe, and other parts of the world to "run to and fro" in its pages, trying to understand it.

But it was not in Daniel's power to "seal the book." God Himself kept it from being understood for many years. "For the words are closed up and sealed till the time of the end" (verse 9).

At the same time, a new method of interpreting Bible prophecy—a new *hermeneutic* (from the Greek word *hermeneuo,* meaning "to interpret")—started to take hold. It would become known as *dispensationalism* and was the theological brainchild of John Nelson Darby, in England, and C. I. Scofield, in America. Dispensationalism represented a departure from historicism, the standard approach to interpreting the prophecies of the Bible and particularly those of Daniel and Revelation.

In the beginning

Since the time of the church fathers in the second and third centuries, prophetic portions of Scripture have been understood to be fulfilled in actual history. This was also the view of the Protestant Reformers. Daniel and Revelation were viewed as complementary books that spanned history from the prophet's day until the end of time, even though considerable portions of the prophecies, especially the second half of Revelation, were yet to be fulfilled in the future.

For example, the statue of Daniel 2 and the wild beasts of Daniel 7 were understood as representing four successive world empires from the time of Daniel onward, spanning over a thousand years from the time of Israel's captivity by Babylon in 605 B.C. through A.D. 476, when the Roman Empire fell. Daniel himself identified the first symbol, the statue's head of gold, as the Babylonian Empire (605–539 B.C.), which would be followed by three other world empires (see Daniel 2:38, 39). Historically, Babylon was followed by Medo-Persia (539–331 B.C.), symbolized by the statue's silver chest and arms. The statue's bronze belly and thighs represented Greece (331–168 B.C.), the next world empire, which was followed in turn by Rome (168 B.C.–A.D. 476), symbolized by the iron legs of the statue. The statue was made of metals of decreasing value, gold, silver, bronze, and iron, which indicated the status of the different world empires. God used a visual image that appealed to the man to whom God first gave the vision,

Nebuchadnezzar, king of Babylon. The beasts of Daniel 7 symbolize the same world powers, but viewed in terms of their relationship to the people of God. Each animal—the lion, the bear, the leopard, the monster—represented a frightening threat.

In the visions of the book of Revelation, the seven churches (Revelation 2; 3) existed in the time of John but may also be viewed as picturing the state of God's people from the first century,* while the events symbolized by the seals (Revelation 5–7) reached at least to the time of Constantine the Great in the fourth century, and the first six trumpets (Revelation 8; 9) would go beyond that, to the centuries of Muslim conquests and Turkish (Ottoman) advances. The various visions—such as the seven churches, the seven seals, the seven trumpets, and so on—cover the history of the church from the first century on, one after the other. That is, these visions picture history from the time of the prophet until the end of time, although each provides different emphases. The visions build on each other and are fulfilled through historical events.

Interpreting the little horn and the antichrist

Historicism was the standard method of interpretation among many early Christians. As early as the second century, Christian interpreters understood that they were living in the days of the fourth beast, which would soon turn into the days of "the little horn." If you read Daniel 7 and 8, you'll see that this "dreadful and terrible" beast, defying similarity to any beast in the animal kingdom, had ten horns—symbols of power. Daniel saw a little horn—a "different" power—slowly rise from among them and in the process plucked up three of the ten horns by the roots (see Daniel 7:7, 8). Daniel was fasci-

* To the Second Coming.

nated by this little horn, because it had eyes "like the eyes of a man" and a mouth "speaking pompous words" (verse 8). It spoke "against the Most High" (verse 25); it grew bigger than the other horns, and made "war against the saints, . . . prevailing against them" (verse 21). It would plan to "change times and law" and the saints would be in the hands of this power "for a time and times and half a time" (verse 25).[2] Clearly, this little horn represents a formidable power opposed to God and His people.

In chapter 8, Daniel gives more detailed descriptions regarding this power. It would grow "toward the south, toward the east, and toward the Glorious Land" (Daniel 8:9). Since the "Glorious Land" refers to Palestine (see Daniel 11:16), it would seem from this description that this power would come from the northwest—in other words, from Rome. The little horn would exalt himself to be "as high as the Prince of the host"—as high as Jesus Himself (Daniel 8:11). And "by *him,* [note that the prophecy is no longer referring to a nameless, inanimate power, but to a power led by a man] the daily sacrifices were taken away, and the place of His [God's] sanctuary was cast down . . . and he cast truth down to the ground" (verses 11, 12; emphasis supplied).

Many early Bible interpreters saw this little horn power of Daniel 7 and 8 as the "man of sin" (2 Thessalonians 2:3) whom Paul speaks about and who displays himself as God. They also identified the little horn with "the beast" found in the book of Revelation (Revelation 13:1) and as "the antichrist" mentioned in the letters of John (1 John 2:18, 22; 4:1–3; 2 John 7). For example, Irenaeus, the second-century bishop of Lyons, France, identified the antichrist as "anxious to be adored as God" and then quoted from 2 Thessalonians, "of whom the apostle speaks" as "the man of sin." He also identified this "man of sin" or "son of perdition" with the little horn of Daniel, and with Revelation's "beast." Here, in his own words, is what Iranaeus had to say, "For when he [the antichrist] is come . . . also shall he deservedly 'be cast into the lake of fire' . . . whose coming John has thus described in the Apocalypse: 'And the beast which I had seen was like a leopard, and his feet as of a bear.' "[3] Regarding the mystic number 666, Irenaeus admonished all "to wait until Rome's division" before attempting to solve the riddle.[4] This was a remarkable insight for someone living in the second century, over two centuries *before* the collapse of Rome.

Tertullian, the second-century pagan ex-lawyer turned Christian apologist, also understood the antichrist mentioned in John's letters to be the beast described in the book of Revelation and the man of sin whom Paul describes. However, in addition, Tertullian pointed out that Rome was delaying the antichrist's appearance. He said, " 'For that day shall not come, unless indeed there first come a falling away,' he [Paul] means indeed of this present empire."[5] Tertullian's "present empire," of course, was the Roman Empire.

Many more references could be cited.[6] The point is that from the earliest days of Christianity, the little horn was understood as the beast of Revelation, the antichrist, and the man of sin. And those ancient Bible students also understood that the delay of the coming of the antichrist and of the great tribulation (Matthew 24:20, 21) was due to activities of the then current Roman Empire. Once the empire would break up into ten powers, the antichrist, or little horn, would rise to power, and with him would come the tribulation.

The Reformers' interpretation

This early church interpretation is consistent with that of

the Reformers, with one difference—the fact that Luther, Calvin, and the other Reformers knew themselves to be living in the actual time of the antichrist and the great tribulation of the 1,260 days of years.

One of the forerunners of the sixteenth-century Reformation was the Englishman, John Wycliffe, known in Christian history as "the Morning Star of the Reformation." Wycliffe was an Oxford scholar with an astute mind. Though not the first one to do so, he boldly identified the pope as the man of sin, the little horn, and the antichrist of prophecy. "Why is it necessary in unbelief to look for another antichrist?" wrote Wycliffe. "In the seventh chapter of Daniel antichrist is forcefully described by a horn arising in the time of the fourth kingdom . . . for so our clergy foresee the lord pope."[7]

We must remember that in spite of such pronouncements Wycliffe, Luther, and the other Reformers were faithful Catholics—before their convictions caused them, in some cases, to break with the established church. In fact, in the Middle Ages, the conviction grew far and wide among thinking believers that the prophecies regarding the antichrist were being fulfilled before their eyes. They felt that Paul's reference to the "falling away," *apostasia* (2 Thessalonians 2:3), had already happened. The corrupt ways of the clergy through bribery and simony—the practice of buying one's way into religious leadership—as well as the adoption of pagan practices and their departure from Bible teachings, the mysticism, and the papal obsession for power at the time, led many Christians to believe they were living in prophetic times and that the antichrist was then present.

In spite of the Reformers' piety and their obvious commitment to the church, their criticisms were too much for the church to take. They were declared heretics, and persecution followed. The Inquisition was established in the twelfth century, and individuals were incarcerated and martyred. Even Girolamo Savonarola, the best-known revivalist preacher of the fifteenth century, was hanged and burned to death because of his interpretations of the book of Revelation and his rejection of papal authority.

By the time Martin Luther came along, these convictions were settled in the minds of many who still had access to the Bible. Luther, a German monk, was a brilliant theologian who carried forward the Protestant Reformation on the wheels of *sola scriptura,* the concept that the Bible *alone* is God's Word and the only rule of faith and practice. Three years after he'd nailed his fateful Ninety-Five Theses to the door of Wittenberg Castle, Luther wrote these words in *The Babylonian Captivity of the Church:* "The papacy is indeed nothing but the kingdom of Babylon and of the true antichrist. For who else is the man of sin and the son of perdition [2 Thessalonians 2:3] than he who multiplies sin and the destruction of souls in the church with his own diatribes and statues, sitting nevertheless in the church like God?"[8] Hard words, indeed!

John Calvin, spiritual forefather of all Reformed denominations, was next. "Some persons think us too severe and censorious when we call the Roman pontiff antichrist. But those who are of this opinion do not consider that they bring the same charge of presumption against Paul himself, after whom we speak and whose language we adopt. . . . I shall briefly show that [Paul's words in 2 Thessalonians 2] are not capable of any other interpretation than that which applies them to the Papacy."[9]

And so it went. John Knox in Scotland, Ulrich Zwingli in Switzerland, John Wesley, Isaac Newton, and Thomas Cramner in England, Jonathan Edwards in America, and many other luminaries came to the same conclusion. Even Roger Williams, considered the first Baptist pastor in America in the seventeenth century, said that the pope was "the pretended Vicar of Christ on earth, who sits as God over the Temple of God, exalting himself not only above all that is called God, but over the souls and consciences of all his vassals, yea over the Spirit of Christ, . . . and God Himself . . . speaking against the God of heaven, thinking to change times and laws; but he is the son of perdition (II Thess. 2)."[10] The well-known Christian document, the Westminster Confession, drafted in 1647, chapter 25, article 6, states, "There is no other head of the church but the Lord Jesus Christ. Nor can the Pope of Rome in any sense be head thereof; but is that antichrist, that man of sin and son of perdition that exalteth himself in the church against Christ and all that is called God."[11]

The Counter-Reformation

The sheer force of the biblical apocalyptic passages that the Reformers used to link the papacy with the antichrist shook the very foundation of the Roman Catholic Church. Feeling threatened, it reacted vigorously to defend itself. The church convened the Council of Trent (1545–1563) in reaction to the doctrines of the Reformers and the claims they were making regarding the church. This council upheld the doctrines of salvation by faith *and* works, transubstantiation (the idea that the Communion bread and wine literally *becomes* the actual flesh and blood of Christ), and purgatory. The council affirmed the basic structure of the church and the Latin Vulgate version of the Bible, including the extra apocryphal books. Other actions of the council placed tradition on par with the Bible as authority for the church's teachings, granted the bishops greater power to supervise all aspects of religious life, and supported the rise of the

Jesuit order, led by Ignatius of Loyola, which was organized along military principles such as discipline, training, and a do-or-die zeal for the pope and the church.[12]

At this time, two Spanish Jesuit scholars, Luis de Alcazar and Francisco Ribera, eager to restore the "ground" lost to Protestantism, began to make their mark in history. Luis de Alcazar revived *preterism,* while Francisco Ribera invented *futurism* as ways to interpret Bible prophecies. The Protestant Reformers were pinning the antichrist label on the pope, using the well-established historicist approach to Bible study. So these two Jesuits countered this interpretation by viewing the Bible prophecies either as having been fulfilled in the far distant past—*preterism*—or as waiting to be fulfilled in the distant future—*futurism.*[13]

In his nine hundred-page commentary on Revelation, de Alcazar (1554–1613) cunningly argued that the antichrist prophecies of Daniel and Revelation had already been fulfilled in the past and that the little horn of Daniel 7 applied to Antiochus IV Epiphanes, who lived in the second century before Christ. The antichrist, he proposed, was an entirely different figure from the little horn and had found its fulfillment in the emperor Nero in the first century. In fact, de Alcazar taught that the whole book of Revelation had been fulfilled in the first six centuries of the Christian era, thus conveniently removing any possibility that either the little horn or the antichrist could refer to the papal institution. Preterism remains a common method of prophetic interpretation in the Catholic Church today.

While de Alcazar picked up the idea of the little horn being the pagan Roman Empire from the Jewish historian Josephus, Francisco Ribera (1554–1591) came up with a new idea. He proposed a literalistic interpretation of the prophecies and projected practically all of them far into the future. For example, instead of the accepted interpretation that the 1,260 prophetic days—or forty-two months or three and a half "times"—represent 1,260 literal years (see Daniel 7:25; 12:7; Revelation 11:2, 3; 12:6, 14; 13:5),[14] Ribera taught that an infidel antichrist, just before the second coming of Christ, would rebuild the temple in Jerusalem, abolish Christianity, be welcomed by the Jews, pretend to be God, and conquer the world—all in the brief span of three and a half years![15]

Ribera's research and conclusions were greatly aided by Roberto Billarmino (1542–1621), an Italian cardinal with great charisma and a thorough education. The result of Billarmino's theological work and public speaking "was the earliest attempt to systematize the various controversies of the time, and made an immense impression throughout Europe," dealing a major initial setback to Protestantism.[16] He concluded that the antichrist could not refer to the pope or to the papacy because the antichrist was an individual and the papacy was a system; that the three and a half "times" were three and a half literal years, but the papacy had existed for centuries; and that the antichrist must rule from Jerusalem, but the papacy did so from Rome.

For the better part of three centuries, the Jesuits did their best to introduce futurism as a method of prophetic interpretation in the universities of Europe. But the Catholic Counter-Reformation simply caused Protestant Bible students to become even more convinced of the correctness of the historicist approach to Bible prophecy. By the early nineteenth century, however, everything began to change.

The rise of modern dispensationalism

America awakened to a major interest in last-day events in the 1800s, in part, as fulfillment of prophecy. The sealed book of Daniel (see Daniel 12:4, 9) became open, as the 1,260-year prophecy came to an end. Daniel's "time of the end" was finally upon the world (see Daniel 8:17; 11:35, 40; 12:4, 9). A millennial fever ignited the hearts of many who now looked for the coming of the Lord. Apocalyptic prophecies became the choice subject for Bible study.

This happened not only in the New World—many people in Europe, South America, and elsewhere also looked to see where they were in the span of history and how the world would end. In this process, however, unbiblical ideas began to filter in.

For example, the Chilean Jesuit priest Manuel de Lacunza y Diaz (1731–1801), wrote a massive study of last-day events and the coming of Christ that made an impact all over the Western world.[17] His view of *eschatology* (the study of the last days) ratified principles of Jesuit futurism—ideas such as the fulfillment of Revelation 4–22 was still in the future, the 144,000 are literal Jews, literal Israel will be gathered and converted during the last-day great Tribulation, and the millennium will be a period of peace on earth when the Old Testament sacrificial system will be re-established in a rebuilt temple in Jerusalem. Lacunza did break from traditional futurism in two significant ways: he taught that Christ's coming will *precede* the millennium (almost everyone at the time believed that Christ would come *after* the millennium), and that the antichrist was not a single individual but a backslidden Christian system.

Lacunza's book was an instant hit with those interested in Bible prophecy. A charismatic and influential Scottish pastor, Edward Irving (1792–1834), co-founder of the Society for the Investigation of Prophecy in London, translated Lacunza's book into English, which then gained wide circulation.[18] Irving eventually joined a small group of men dissatisfied with the spiritual condition of the Protestant church in Ireland and England. There were a number of such groups, the best known was located in Plymouth and became knows as "the Plymouth Brethren." They gained a reputation as dissenters from the Church of England and from traditional Protestantism in general.

One of these Plymouth Brethren was pastor and lawyer John Nelson Darby (1800–1882). Darby was deeply frustrated with the church. He saw a distressing disconnect between the early church in the book of Acts and the current Protestant experience. C. Norman Kraus, an expert on this subject, has written, "It should be carefully noted that Darby's first and basic dissent was not on the question of eschatology, but on the doctrine of the Church. . . . It was his intent to make a wider church unity possible through a nondenominational approach."[19]

Darby's dissatisfaction with the church led him to view it more as an accident of history rather than the continuum of God's people throughout history. This led him to understand salvation history in terms of "dispensations" which would ultimately prove profoundly influential in the way many people today interpret Scripture.

Pastor C. I. Scofield (1843–1921) later refined Darby's ideas and popularized them through his *Scofield Reference Bible* (1909 and 1917). The *New Scofield Reference Bible* appeared in 1967. Scofield defined a dispensation as "a period of time during which man is tested in respect of obedience to some *specific* revelation of the will of God."[20] Thus, he divided salvation history into seven dispensations: (1) innocence: Adam and Eve in Eden, (2) conscience or moral responsibility: the antediluvian world, (3) human government: between the

Flood and Abraham, (4) promise: the patriarchal age, (5) law: Israel, (6) church: the age of grace, and (7) kingdom: the millennium.

In addition, Irving taught the idea of a two-phase return of Christ, one secret and the other visible. He was influenced to think that way by Margaret MacDonald, a sixteen-year-old parishioner in his church who, in April 1830, claimed to have received a series of visions showing that in the last days, the church will be raptured to escape the Tribulation! This was not entirely shocking to those close to the situation, since for several years Irving's church had been experiencing charismatic phenomena such as speaking in tongues or being "slain in the Spirit."

The rest is history. In 1970, Hal Lindsey popularized futurist concepts in his wildly popular book *The Late Great Planet Earth*. The fact that he mistakenly predicted the rapture to take place in 1981, and then in 1988, did not dampen the interest people had for this unique interpretation of prophecy. In the 1990s, the sixteen-volume *Left Behind* series of novels by Tim LaHaye and Jerry B. Jenkins sold over sixty-five million copies, and millions also watched the various movies made based on the book's contents. For decades now, futurism has found a vigorous academic advocate in the Dallas Theological Seminary, the largest center for pastoral training in the United States, graduating hundreds of ministers and Bible teachers every year.

Implications for Christians today

Why is it that futurism, dispensations, a secret rapture, Bible literalism, the dichotomy between Israel and the church, and other concepts foreign to careful biblical scholarship have been so well received by so many sincere believers?

The Story of a Wrong Approach

An extreme form of biblical literalism has led to an emphasis on prophetic *words* rather than prophetic *meaning* (remember from chapter 1 that inspiration works on the mind of the writer more than it does directly on the pen). The idea of various dispensations broke up the biblical concept that God has only one way of salvation for every human being. It created the so-called gap theory, in the interpretation of Daniel's seventy-week prophecy, giving way to a new, nonbiblical picture of the role of Israel at the end of time. Events related to the return of Christ are thoroughly muddled with concepts that are relatively new in the span of Christian history and that are foreign to biblical evidence.

Perhaps a key attraction is the notion that persons of faith will be spared pain and suffering at the end. But as we saw in the previous chapter, this is inconsistent with the story of the Bible. God's people will hang on to Him while facing Tribulation. Perhaps the reason for the popularity of these unbiblical notions of prophetic interpretation has to do with Scofield's Bible notes and the rising fundamentalism seen in America in the early twentieth century. This movement was a valiant step to remain true to the Bible in the wake of increasing liberal tendencies and the social gospel. But the perceived simplicity of taking every passage of Scripture literally, whether warranted or not, has opened the door to a certain carelessness in Bible study, focusing on the mere words God said, while doing away with the effort to understand what He actually meant.

Because of these misdirections, it is important to faithfully practice sound principles of prophetic interpretation in order to discern truth from error. And that's where we'll go next. Do not be discouraged in any way. No one needs to hold a PhD in biblical interpretation in order to understand the Bible correctly. God gave us His Word for all to understand. Men and women of faith have apprehended God's Word throughout history by prayerfully reading it and seeking to do His will. We must approach the Bible with humility and with an open mind, seeking to leave behind preconceived ideas. The Bible, after all, is "profitable for doctrine, for reproof, for correction, for instruction in righteousness, that the man of God may be complete, thoroughly equipped for every good work" (2 Timothy 3:16, 17).

CHAPTER 4
GENERAL PRINCIPLES OF BIBLICAL INTERPRETATION

As every thinking person knows, it is the context that determines the meaning of words. And this also applies to the study of the Bible. When someone says, "You've got to be kidding!" he is really saying, "That is hard to believe!" He is not really wondering whether you have told a joke. Real communication happens when everyone understands what the speaker actually *means*. Words are only tools, and they can be used in many different ways. Understanding the meaning behind those words is what matters.

Sometimes we don't understand what people are saying, because we don't listen very well. Before they finish saying what they have in mind, we begin to formulate in our mind a rebuttal. We may assume the person is saying something he or she does not mean at all. We do the same with the Bible. We assume it is teaching some things that it is not teaching, and vice versa, simply because our presuppositions get in the way. We are not really listening, though we think we are. This even happens with well-trained Bible scholars.[1]

We don't want to misinterpret what God is teaching us in His Word, do we? So, let's review some general principles of biblical interpretation, and later we will add a few principles that are especially applicable to end-time prophecies.

Principle 1: Spiritual things are spiritually discerned

This is where we must begin. Paul made it quite clear: "No one knows the things of God except the Spirit of God. . . . The natural man does not receive the things of the Spirit of God, for they are foolishness to him; nor can he know them, because they are spiritually discerned" (1 Corinthians 2:11, 14).

The Bible teaches that we have been created as multidimensional people—physically, emotionally, intellectually, and spiritually. Created in God's image, a human being can respond to what God says and does, unlike the beasts of the field. But our natural tendency is to misinterpret God, to miss His cues. We do so because our natures are corrupted through sin, and that distorts our perception of reality. "There is a way that seems right to a man, but its end is the way of death" (Proverbs 14:12). Our sinful nature superimposes itself over the wisdom of God, and we end up thinking we know more than He does.

What we need, then, is humility. When we choose to surrender ourselves before God, the way is open for Him to communicate more clearly with us. The natural barriers are removed. He Himself suggested this very thing, when He said, "If anyone wills to do His [the Father's] will, he shall know concerning the doctrine, whether it is from God" (John 7:17). Doctrine means teaching. What God wants to teach us depends on our willingness to actually follow through with what He says. That calls for humble surrender to Him. If my will, my spirit, yields to Him, I will then understand what He wishes to convey.

There is an approach to scriptural interpretation, called "higher criticism," that violates this principle. Basically, this method of interpretation seeks to study the Bible in the same way other ancient documents are studied—clinically, devoid of faith, detached from personal surrender. It is no wonder that such theologians do not believe in miracles or that they claim the prophecies were actually written *after* their fulfillment. Since critical scholars don't see anything supernatural in other ancient documents, those miraculous or prophetic sections of Scripture are either discarded or reinterpreted.

This method of Bible study is practiced by scores of Bible scholars who write books that end up in seminaries and influence many pastors who end up teaching these views as the Word of God to unsuspecting church members. And many believers, sad to say, depend almost entirely on the word of their pastor to understand what the Bible teaches.

This is not to say that no scholar can be trusted. Many scholars are reliable Bible expositors, and their knowledge and insight can be very helpful. But if anyone is to interpret the Scriptures correctly, he or she must be willing to surrender self, his or her pre-conceived ideas, and his or her will to God. Then, the Spirit will illuminate his or her mind to understand the things of God.

Principle 2: The Bible is Christ-centered

The theme of the Bible is Jesus, plain and simple. The entire Old Testament is about the Messiah to come, starting with God's promise to Adam and Eve in the Garden (see Genesis 3:15). The New Testament is about the Messiah's teaching, ministry, and sacrifice, and His promise to come again. Christ Himself told the unbelieving Pharisees, "You search the Scriptures, for in them you think you have eternal life; and these are they which testify of Me" (John 5:39). Salvation, Jesus said, does not come by the academic study of God's Word. It comes by the Person whom that Word reveals—the Son of God.

The Old Testament also revealed Jesus by "types," or symbols, in the form of persons, events, or institutions that give glimpses of His character, His life, and His way of salvation. Christ, then, is the "Antitype"—the fulfillment—of such Old Testament types. For example, Jesus was the true Bread from heaven that gives eternal life, while the manna in the wilderness was a type, or symbol, of that reality (see John 6:47–51). Christ declared Himself to be "greater than the temple," "greater than Jonah," and "greater than Solomon" (Matthew 12:6, 41, 42). That means He was greater than the most sacred place of worship and its high priest, greater than the most successful prophet in Israel, and greater than the greatest king of Israel. The high priest, Jonah, and Solomon were types of Christ, forerunners of His glory.

The entire sanctuary and its ministry was also a type of Christ. The sacrificial lamb was a type of Christ as a substitute for the death of sinners (see John 1:29). The priest represented Christ's ministry on the sinner's behalf (see Hebrews 8:1–6). The altar was a symbol of Christ's sacrifice (see Matthew 23:18, 19). The veil was a type of Christ's flesh (see Hebrews 10:19, 20). And so on. The annual festivals connected with the sanctuary and temple ministries—called sabbaths—were also a shadow of Jesus Christ and of His work (see Colossians 2:16, 17). Passover stood for Calvary, Pentecost—the day when Moses received God's commandments at Mount Sinai—became the day when Christ's church received the Holy Spirit, and the Feast of Tabernacles represented the day when God's people would be gathered to Him in heaven.[2]

Even the most mysterious book in the Bible, Revelation, is about Jesus as its opening words indicate, "The Revelation of Jesus Christ, which God gave Him to show His servants" (Revelation 1:1). This fact should never be far from the mind of the Bible student: the entire Bible is about Jesus.

Principle 3: The Bible interprets itself

This principle of the Bible interpreting itself was practiced by the Reformers of the sixteenth century. They called it *sola scriptura*—Scripture alone. By this, they meant not only that they would make the Bible, and not church tradition, the sole rule of faith and practice for the Christian, but that the Bible is its own interpreter. The Christian church of that time had come to the conclusion that it was unsafe to leave matters of biblical interpretation in the hands of common people. The Bible was too difficult to understand. To solve that problem, they placed biblical interpretation in the hands of the pope, along with the magisterium, or the scholars of the church. This meant that no Christian could read and understand the Bible without the aid of the church. The Reformers said, "No!" The Reformers said that the Bible was written as God's letter for all His children, and each can understand it, for the keys to its interpretation are within the Word itself. The Bible interprets itself.

Jesus Himself believed in this principle. On the morning of His resurrection, two of His disciples were walking to Emmaus, a town seven miles from Jerusalem. They were discussing the weekend's events—the Crucifixion and the reports of Jesus' resurrection. They were bitterly discouraged, for they never imagined the Messiah would be killed (see Luke 24:13–24). Jesus approached them without being recognized and listened to their tale of woe. Obviously, He wanted to tell them that He was alive and had been victorious over death itself. He could have performed a miracle to open their eyes or He could have shown the glory of His resurrection to wow them into joy. But He didn't do any of that.

Christ knew that "faith comes by hearing, and hearing by the word of God" (Romans 10:17). Miracles do not generate faith; they can only confirm faith. Jesus wanted those two disciples to come to believe in God's plan and see it for themselves. So, "beginning at Moses and all the Prophets, He expounded to them in all the Scriptures the things concerning Himself" (Luke 24:27). He first led them to what Moses, in the first five books of the Bible, said about the Messiah. Then He pointed them to what other Old Testament prophets had said about His life and ministry—perhaps quoting texts in Isaiah, Daniel, Micah, and Haggai. He did this "in all the Scriptures."

Instead of giving them a direct word of knowledge and truth, He let the Bible explain itself, point by point. As a result, they understood that the Bible had predicted the events of the past weekend, and assurance and joy followed. Later, they exclaimed, "Did not our heart burn within us while He talked with us on the road, and while He opened the Scriptures to us?" (verse 32).

In my work as a Bible teacher, I have seen scores of men, women, and even children, come to understand God's Word for themselves without the aid of external sources, without the interpretation arrived at by others. The Bible can be understood, for God intended it for all of us, not just for some of us.

The key is to start with the simpler texts and go on from there, letting the Bible answer for itself. Take, for instance, the woman of Revelation 12. Who is she? Revelation 12:1 says, "Now a great sign appeared in heaven: a woman clothed with the sun, with the moon under her feet, and on her head a garland of twelve stars." One thing is clear right from the start: the "woman" is symbolic of something else, because no woman can actually be clothed with the sun and have the moon under her feet. So, this is clearly symbolic language. What, then, does she stand for?

A number of times in the Old Testament, God compares His people, Israel, to a "woman." For example, "For your Maker is your husband, the LORD of hosts is His name; and your Redeemer is the Holy One of Israel. . . . For the LORD has called you like a woman forsaken and grieved in spirit, like a youthful wife" (Isaiah 54:5, 6). Or, "I have likened the daughter of Zion [another name for Israel] to a lovely and delicate woman" (Jeremiah 6:2). In the New Testament, the apostles continued with the same analogy. Paul wrote about the church as a woman engaged to be married: "I am jealous for you with godly jealousy. For I have betrothed you to one husband, that I may present you as a chaste virgin to Christ" (2 Corinthians 11:2). Even in the book of Revelation, John called the church "the bride" (Revelation 22:17).

If the woman of Revelation 12 is Christ's church, can the Bible also tell us the meaning of her being "clothed with the sun" and with "the moon under her feet"? The easier of the two would be the "sun" since that object appears so much more often in the Bible than does the moon. The last Old Testament prophet has the key. Writing about the end of the world and the coming of Christ, Malachi said, "For behold, the day is coming, burning like an oven, and all the proud, yes, all who do wickedly will be stubble. And the day which is coming shall burn them up. . . . But to you who fear My name the Sun of Righteousness shall arise with healing in His wings" (Malachi 4:1, 2). So, the "sun" is Jesus, the Deliverer of His people at the end of the world. Does this mean, then, that the church is clothed with Jesus? Yes! Paul said Christians should "put on Christ" (Galatians 3:27) and also that they should "put on the new man who is renewed in knowledge according to the image of Him who created him" (Colossians 3:10).

So, the woman is the church clothed with Jesus. What about "the moon under her feet"? This we can figure out. We know the moon can be seen only as it reflects the light of the sun. And nothing in the Bible reflects Jesus more faithfully than the Old Testament sanctuary system of types and ceremonies. Such types were eclipsed by Christ Himself in the New Testament when He fulfilled all that these symbols foretold about Him and His work. Then it follows that the moon basically stands for the Bible in the Old Testament. Jesus said, "And these [the Old Testament Scriptures] are they which testify of Me" (John 5:39).

The Bible interprets itself when we allow it to speak for itself. Obviously, the more we know about what the Bible says, the easier it may be to discern the meaning of difficult passages. But this cannot be done haphazardly. Each Bible text must be seen in its true context. And that is our next principle.

Principle 4: Context is paramount

There is an old axiom applicable to Bible study: "A text without context is a pretext." That is, any interpretation of a Bible text that ignores its context—what precedes it, what follows it, what the author is trying to say in that section of Scripture—can lead to the pretext of pushing a preconceived idea. Sometimes people think that each isolated word, taken literally, will give the true meaning of the text. But that is nonsense. Words make sentences, sentences paragraphs, paragraphs chapters, and chapters make books of the Bible. Each word and sentence is surrounded by a context that must be taken into consideration if one wants to know the true meaning of what God is saying through the prophet or apostle. The *etymology* (origin and derivation) of a word is not all that needs to be considered; we must also take into account how that author uses it and/or how the Bible, in general, uses it. Take, for example, the following passage from the apostle Paul:

> But I do not want you to be ignorant, brethren, concerning those who have fallen asleep, lest you sorrow as others who have no hope. For if we believe that Jesus died and rose again, even so God will bring with Him those who sleep in Jesus. For this we say to you by the word of the Lord, that we who are alive and remain until the coming of the Lord will by no means precede those who are asleep. For the Lord Himself will descend from heaven with a shout, with the voice of an archangel, and with the trumpet of God. And the dead in Christ will rise first. Then we who are alive and remain shall be caught up together with them in the clouds to meet the Lord in the air. And thus we shall always be with the Lord. Therefore comfort one another with these words (1 Thessalonians 4:13–18).

We could use this passage to rectify a number of things people make it say that are not so. But we'll just focus on one thing at this time. Many sincere Christians believe this passage teaches a secret rapture of the church. Let's see what we can find out from the text's context.

First, the apostle Paul addresses the concern some Thessalonians had that friends were dying and Christ had not returned yet. He assured them they didn't have to worry about their friends' salvation, for they had died in the hope that they would be resurrected when Jesus comes. How would this happen? Christ said that He *Himself* will descend from heaven (verse 16). Paul emphasizes this. So, Jesus will not be sending a proxy, a deputy, to pick us up; He Himself will come! This is corroborated by other texts in the New Testament, such as John 14:1–3, in which Jesus tells His disciples He will be the one coming back, and Acts 1:9–11, in which the angels tell the disciples that "this same Jesus" will "come in like manner" as He went to heaven. Just as He ascended in the clouds, He will descend in the clouds.

In addition, Paul adds that Christ's descent from heaven will be accompanied "with a shout, with the voice of an archangel, and with the trumpet of God" (1 Thessalonians 4:16). That does not sound like anything secret, let alone a secret rapture. It does sound like it will be noisy, very loud—and visible, based on other texts about His coming (see Revelation 1:7; Matthew 24:30).

But the reason some believe this passage refers to a secret rapture is because of the expression "caught up"—"we who are alive . . . shall be caught up together with them in the clouds." The Greek word translated as "caught up" is *harpazo,* which means "to snatch away." It does not mean "to disappear," as some interpret it. This "snatching away" is not in the context of a secret, "spiritual" coming of Christ. It is in the context of the resurrection. Paul makes this abundantly clear. "The dead in Christ will rise first. Then we who are alive and remain shall be caught up together with them in the clouds to meet the Lord in the air" (1 Thessalonians 4:16, 17).

So, there will be a *rapture* (from the Latin word *rapio,* a translation of the Greek word *harpazo*), but it will not be secret, at least according to this text. Neither will it take place before the return of Christ or before the Tribulation. We will be "caught up" when Jesus Himself comes and the first resurrection takes place.[3]

If this is so clear, why do people still think this text teaches a secret rapture? Perhaps because they misread what Paul says just two verses later: "For you yourselves know perfectly that the day of the Lord so comes as a thief in the night" (1 Thessalonians 5:2). They read this text and believe that "thief in the night" means "secret." But is that what Paul says or means?

Again, let's look at the context. Verse 3 explains verse 2. "For when they say, 'Peace and safety!' then sudden destruction comes upon them, as labor pains upon a pregnant woman. And they shall not escape" (verse 3). In other words, when people feel invulnerable to thieves—feeling safe and at peace—that's when destruction comes suddenly. So, the expression "thief in the night" speaks of the *suddenness,* or the unexpectedness of the thief's appearance—not that he comes secretly. The coming of Jesus is as sudden and unexpected "as labor pains" in "a pregnant woman." There is nothing secret about labor pains, but there is everything sudden about them. Even though she may anticipate the contractions, when they come, it is as if she had not known what to expect. They are really something!

A text without context is a pretext to teach and say what the text never intended to say. Entire philosophical or theological systems can be built around misunderstandings such as this. You can imagine how dangerous this is! So, it's *very* important to seek the meaning of the text by carefully reading what the author intended to say.

Principle 5: Prophecies can be conditional

A conditional prophecy is a biblical prediction whose fulfillment depends on the action or reaction of human beings. For example, there are prophecies of prosperity or doom to God's people, but their fulfillment is tied to His people's faithfulness. Sometimes, conditional prophecies are preceded by the word *if* at the very start: "If you are willing and obedient, you shall eat the good of the land" (Isaiah 1:19). The promise of abundance from the land is tied to Israel's obedience.

Of course, not all prophecies in the Bible are conditional. Apocalyptic prophecies—those prophecies related to the end times—are not conditional. They simply foretell what will happen. But many prophecies in the Old Testament are tied to conditions. A clear example is the prophecy of the destruction of Nineveh. "Yet forty days, and Nineveh shall be overthrown," proclaimed the prophet (Jonah 3:4). But the citizens of Nineveh turned to the Lord. They "believed God, proclaimed a fast" and humbled themselves before Him. "Then God saw their works, that they turned from their evil way; and God relented from the disaster that He had said He would bring upon them, and He did not do it" (verses 5, 10).

Many of the Old Testament prophecies about Israel are conditional. Moses made that clear. "If you diligently obey the voice of the LORD your God, to observe carefully all His commandments which I command you today, . . . the LORD your God will set you high above all nations of the earth. . . . But . . . if you do not obey the voice of the LORD your God, to observe carefully all His commandments . . . all these curses will come upon you and overtake you" (Deuteronomy 28:1, 15). Israel's prosperity was tied to its faithfulness to God's covenant. However, Israel proved to be unfaithful. The Israelites were finally exiled to Babylon, to live among the gods of their choosing.

In His great mercy, God gave Israel a second chance. He opened the way for Jews to return to their land after the seventy years of captivity in Babylon were fulfilled (see Jeremiah 25:12–14; Ezra 1:1–2:1). Again, He made promises to them like the covenant promises He had given them in the past. But Israel failed again, and both Greeks and Romans overtook their land. "These [Old Testament] prophecies that look forward to a restored Jewish state in the land of Palestine were made either prior to the release of the Jews from their Babylonian captivity, or during the rebuilding days soon after their return. God would have fulfilled these promises if Israel had been faithful and obedient to the conditions stated."[4] God promised them no third chance.

Many Bible students today anticipate that the nation of Israel will return to great glory, but they forget that the conditions to Israel's success were not fulfilled. All those glorious promises will not be fulfilled to a literal Israelite nation, because they simply do not meet the conditions.

It is the same with us today. God promises salvation for those who will accept Jesus. "He who has the Son has life; he who does not have the Son of God does not have life" (1 John 5:12). The condition is clear: Jesus being in my life! If that condition is not met, God will not save anyone against his or her will. But when the condition is met, the fulfillment of His promise will surely follow!

CHAPTER 5
THE BOOKS OF DANIEL AND REVELATION

Nowhere in Scripture is *apocalyptic* (end-of-the-world) prophecy more obvious than in the books of Daniel and Revelation. The multiple use of symbols, the time prophecies, the stark contrast between good and evil, the sweeping view of history—it's all there in these two very complementary books.

In Revelation, we find the consummation of some of the concepts introduced by Daniel. For instance, in Daniel, King Nebuchadnezzar erects a statue of gold, ninety feet tall, in Babylon and orders all royal employees to come and worship it. Failure to do so would result in death by fire (see Daniel 3:1–6). In Revelation, an image is also set up, and the whole world is commanded to worship it or die (see Revelation 13:11–16). Whereas in Daniel the command to worship the statue was national in scope, in Revelation it is international.

In Daniel, we find four beasts coming out of the sea, representing four political powers (see Daniel 7:2–7). A lion with eagles' wings (Babylon), a bear raised on one side (Medo-Persia), a four-headed leopard with wings (Greece), and a dreadful-looking beast with ten horns and iron teeth (Rome).[1] In Revelation, the same beasts are also seen coming out of the sea, but this time as a single, amalgamated, dreadful beast with ten horns and having characteristics of each of the four found in Daniel (see Revelation 13:1, 2). And so the similarities continue. In Daniel, the issue of judgment is prominent (see Daniel 5:17–28; 7:9–14, 21, 22). In Revelation, symbolic Babylon is judged (see Revelation 17; 18). In Daniel, the sanctuary ministry is highlighted (see Daniel 8:9–14), and in Revelation, the sanctuary appears as the introduction to all the major visions (see Revelation 1:10–20; 4:1–5; 8:2–6; 11:19; 15:1–16:1; 16:18–17:3; 19:1–10; 21:5–11).[2]

The book of Daniel

The book of Daniel was written by the prophet of that name, a member of the Jewish nobility who was taken captive by the Babylonians in the invasion of Jerusalem in 605 B.C. Daniel's name means "God is my judge," and judgment is a major theme in the book. Daniel and his friends did not compromise their faith as exiles in Babylon, but were found to be skilled and trustworthy while serving in administrative positions. Daniel served at the highest levels of power for both Babylonian, and later, Medo-Persian kings (see Daniel 1:19–21; 6:1–3).

The earliest Christian expositors of Daniel's prophecies took a historicist position, agreeing that the book was written in the sixth century B.C. and that the symbols (metals, beasts, etc.) representing the various kingdoms were successively fulfilled in history.

Subsequently, higher-criticism scholars, who did not believe in the predictive nature of prophecy, taught that Daniel was written in the second century B.C., in response to the harassment of the Jews by the Seleucid king Antiochus IV Epiphanes. This understanding is also implied in the *apocryphal* (spurious, noncanonical) book of 1 Maccabees, leading some to believe that Daniel was written after the facts predicted had taken place. (Incidentally, this view also does away with identifying the little horn of Daniel 7 and 8 with the religious phase of Rome.) However, the earlier date for the writing of the book is supported by the sections written in the Aramaic language (Daniel 2:4–7:28). The Aramaic found in Daniel belongs to the imperial phase of the language (around 600–500 B.C.), in use at the time the prophet lived. By the time of Antiochus, however, there were noticeable linguistic changes in the language—changes that are not evident in the book.[3]

Characteristics of Daniel

The book of Daniel is clearly apocalyptic, full of symbols, time prophecies leading to the end times, and contrasting pictures between the forces of good and evil. It can be easily divided into two parts: prophecy and history. Roughly, the first half of the book is historical narrative (chapters 1, 3–6) while the last half is made up of prophetic visions (chapters 2, 7–12). The purpose of the book is to remind readers that the Most High God rules over the kingdoms of men.

A clear feature of the book is the progressive nature of its four visions. In Daniel 2, the vision is about a metal statue made of gold, silver, bronze, and iron, with feet of iron and clay. These statue sections, made of different metals, represent the kingdoms of Babylon, Medo-Persia, Greece, and Rome in succession, followed by the eventual breakup of the Roman Empire into ten nations.

In chapter 7, the same four kingdoms appear, this time as ferocious beasts, followed by a "little horn" power that arises in the midst of the ten horns and displaces three of them. The main focus of chapter 8 is the role of this little horn that came after the fall of the Roman Empire. In the vision and its explanation found in Daniel 8 and 9, the sequence begins with Medo-Persia (Daniel 8:20), since at this time Babylon was already in the past, and focuses on the role of the little horn, the power following the Roman Empire. Finally, in the last vision (Daniel 10–12:3), minute historical details are given in advance regarding kings and political intrigue from the Medo-Persian kings on through the succeeding world powers. In this vision, a section has not been historically fulfilled to date: Daniel 11:40–45.

Daniel's last visions took place at the end of his life. He was nearly ninety years old when God commanded him to conclude his prophetic work and "seal the book until the time of the end" (Daniel 12:4). Readers can expect the book's vision mysteries to be revealed at that time.

The book of Revelation

According to long-standing Christian tradition going back to the second century,[4] the book of Revelation, also called the Apocalypse, was written by John the Beloved, a disciple of Jesus, who also wrote the Gospel of John and three short letters that appear in the New Testament. John was the last surviving member of the original twelve disciples, and, apparently, was ministering in Ephesus when he was banished to Patmos (see Revelation 1:9).

John must have been in his nineties when Emperor Domitian (A.D. 81–96), the first Roman ruler demanding *live* emperor worship, arrested John. Up to this point, Roman emperors had been worshiped as deities but only *after* their deaths. Domitian opposed Christianity, charging Christians with "atheism" and "Jewish customs," and began a persecution against them in A.D. 95. He condemned John to death by putting him in a caldron of oil, but God miraculously spared the apostle's life. John was then banished to Patmos, a penal colony off the coast of Asia Minor (today's Turkey). After Domitian died, Nerva, the next emperor, released John from prison, and he returned to Ephesus.

Revelation complements and unveils the book of Daniel specifically, but it also complements the entire Old Testament. Whereas Daniel begins with a promise that the climax of the first vision must happen in the last days (Daniel 2:45), Revelation begins with the assurance that such things "must shortly take place" (Revelation 1:1).

In addition, Revelation is the consummation of the entire Scriptures. That is why it is important not to study Revelation in isolation from the rest of the Bible. Even though Revelation repeats no Bible text word for word, there are at least six hundred Old Testament allusions in its 404 verses. Scholars note that John must not have used the Septuagint (abbreviated LXX), the customary Greek Old Testament translation of the time, because his Greek sounds more like Hebrew! The apostle must have "preferred to work directly from the original Hebrew or from popular Aramaic translations."[5]

Characteristics of Revelation

The book of Revelation is also divided into two parts: a historical part and an eschatological part. The first fourteen chapters, mostly historical, deal with the broad sweep of Christian history from the New Testament (about A.D. 100), showing the vulnerability of the church over the centuries. The last eight chapters are eschatological, that is, they pertain to the very end times. These are mostly judgment chapters, showing God's final triumph over evil.

The subjects of these two sections basically coincide with the book's twofold purpose as stated in the beginning: "The Revelation of Jesus Christ . . . to show to His servants—things which must shortly take place" (Revelation 1:1). That is, the book reveals Christ in a way not seen before, not even in the Gospels, giving us assurance that God is in control of His church and salvation history. In addition, it foretells future events that will climax with Christ's victorious return and triumph over His enemies. The focus of Revelation is the struggles and triumphs of God's church between the time of John and the end of time.

It doesn't take long for the student of Revelation to discover several significant "sevens" in the book. The number seven is understood to be a symbol of completion or perfection, and Revelation includes what could be called "the four big sevens"—the seven churches (chapters 2 and 3), the seven seals (chapter 6), the seven trumpets (chapters 8 and 9), and the seven last plagues (chapter 16).[6]

Most Revelation scholars recognize the structure of Revelation as a *chiasm*. A *chiastic* structure is like a pyramid and is typical of Hebrew thought patterns. Whereas in Western literature books tend to build toward a climax at the end, in Hebrew thinking, the climax comes at the middle, at the heart of the chiasm, with both sides of the pyramid building up to it and paralleling across it. There are several possible ways to see the chiasm in Revelation.[7] For the sake of simplicity and consistency, we could see a chiasm with a prologue, an epilogue, and seven sections:

Prologue: Blessing for those who read the prophecies (1:1–8)
  1. The Seven Churches: The church militant (1:9–3:22)
    2. The Seven Seals: The church's struggles (4:1–8:1)
      3. The Seven Trumpets: Judgments against the church's enemies (8:2–11:18)
        4. The Great Conflict: Warfare over God's church (11:19–14:20)
        5. The Seven Plagues: Sentences against the church's enemies (15:1–18:24)

6. The End and the Millennium: The church at rest (19:1–21:4)
7. The New Jerusalem: The church triumphant (21:5–22:5)
Epilogue: Blessing for those who keep the prophecies (22:6–22)

Since the climax in a chiastic structure is at the center, the greatest issue in Revelation is the warfare over God's people. And the heart of the warfare is over worship allegiance: whether to worship God the Creator (Revelation 14:6) or the beast and his image (Revelation 14:9–11). This is a key point to keep in mind as we study this book. At the end of time, worship allegiance will be the subject of Armageddon, earth's greatest and ultimate battle.

It is significant also to note that many of the sevens in Revelation come in groups of four of one kind followed by three of another kind. For example, the first four seals are four horses, while the next three seals do not have horses. The first four trumpets as well as the first four plagues affect the earth, the sea, the rivers, and the sun, while the last three are of a different nature. Even in the chiastic structure itself we see this four-three arrangement: the first four sections have already been fulfilled historically, while the last three sections are yet to be fulfilled. Chapters 13 and 14 of Revelation, for reasons I will explain later, are taking place now, at this current historical time.

A unique characteristic of the book of Revelation is the way it consistently points to heavenly things. It does this in two ways. One is through a picture of the heavenly sanctuary in the introduction of each section. The other is through specific interludes—purposeful interruptions to what is being described—found in most sections.[8] After each interlude, John goes back to the subject in question with what can be called an eschatological culmination.

Below are two tables showing the seven sections of the book in more detail.

Historical Half

1. Seven Churches: The Church Militant	2. Seven Seals: The Church's Struggles	3. Seven Trumpets: Judgments Against the Church's Enemies	4. The Great Conflict: Warfare Over God's Church
Sanctuary Intro: Jesus walks among the candlesticks (1:9–22)	Sanctuary Intro: Scene at the throne room in heaven (4:1–5:14)	Sanctuary Intro: Angel with the golden censer at the altar (8:2–6)	Sanctuary Intro: The ark of the covenant is seen in heaven (11:19)
Activity: God communicates to the seven churches (2; 3)	Activity: God reveals the trials and tribulations of the church through the seals (6)	Activity: God describes the condemnation of the enemies of the church through the trumpets (8:7–9:21)	Activity: God outlines the persecution of the church by the dragon, sea beast, and land beast (12; 13)
No Interlude	Interlude: The saints are sealed before the end (7:1–8:1)	Interlude: The witnesses minister, and the little book is open (10:1–11:13)	Interlude: The last messages are proclaimed (14:1–13)
No Eschatological Culmination	Eschatological Culmination: Heaven is silent (8:1)	Eschatological Culmination: Heaven and earth become Christ's (11:14–18)	Eschatological Culmination: Christ comes to reap the earth (14:14–20)

Eschatological Half

5. Seven Plagues and Babylon: Sentences against the church's enemies	6. The End and the Millennium: The church at rest	7. The New Jerusalem: The church triumphant
Intro: Intercession finished in the heavenly temple (15:1–16:1)	Intro: The multitude in heaven condemns Babylon and exalts the Lamb (19:1–10)	Intro: Promise for things new (21:5–8)
Activity: God sentences judgment upon His enemies, including Babylon, through the last plagues (16:2–14, 16; 17:1–18:3, 9–20)	Activity: God forecasts details about the coming of Christ and start of the millennium (19:11–20:5)	Activity: God describes heaven and the New Jerusalem (21:9–22:5)
Interlude: Appeal to be ready for Christ's return by coming out of Babylon (16:15; 18:4–8)	Interlude: Blessing over those belonging to the first resurrection (20:6)	No Interlude
Eschatological Culmination: Result from Babylon's judgment (18:21–24)	Eschatological Culmination: Final sentence for Satan and his followers (20:7–21:4)	No Eschatological Culmination

One of the most exciting journeys any Bible student may undertake is the study of these amazing prophecies of Daniel and Revelation. In this small study, we cannot go through major portions of these books, although hints and ideas are offered throughout for the reader to take up more thoroughly on his or her own.

We will, however, do a more careful study of at least one of these prophecies. But, first, let's look at a few more principles of interpretation applicable to just this type of prophetic book—apocalyptic prophecy.

Read on. The best is yet to come.

CHAPTER 6
PRINCIPLES FOR THE STUDY OF APOCALYPTIC PROPHECY

The word *apocalyptic* comes from the Greek word *apokalypsis,* which means, literally, "removal of the covering," or "revelation." *Revelation* is the English word used to name the last book of the Bible. However, *biblical apocalyptic* is a specific genre in literature that includes prophetic portions of Scripture laden with symbolism, dealing with broad issues of universal importance, emphasizing the conflict between good and evil, dividing time and history into eras, and focusing on the end times and life after death.[1] This definition particularly describes the books of Daniel and Revelation, as well as portions of the books of Ezekiel and Zechariah.

The unique nature of apocalyptic prophecy requires some specific principles of interpretation beyond the general principles of biblical interpretation that we examined in chapter 4. Here are some necessary principles to keep in mind in order to correctly interpret this particular aspect of biblical truth.

Principle 1: Symbols have concrete explanations

Apocalyptic prophecies are characterized by highly symbolic language and include such figures as lambs, dragons, strange beasts, women, horns, and many others. In addition, proper names—whether geographic or ethnic—are also symbolic, such as Babylon, Egypt, the Euphrates River, and Mount

Zion. Each of these symbols stands for a corresponding concrete explanation.

The book of Revelation was intentionally written in this kind of symbolic language. John begins with these words: "The Revelation of Jesus Christ, which God gave Him. . . . And He sent and *signified it* by His angel to His servant John" (Revelation 1:1; emphasis supplied). Jesus Himself coded Revelation with signs or symbols.

Symbols cannot be understood literally. For instance, a beast with seven heads, ten horns, that looks like a leopard with bearlike feet and the mouth of a lion (see Revelation 13:1, 2) is clearly not anything found anywhere in the animal kingdom. Clearly, this is a symbol of some complex entity.

The following table shows a few symbols found in the book of Revelation:

Symbol	Concrete, Literal Meaning	Where Found
The dragon	Satan, "that serpent of old, called the Devil and Satan"	Revelation 12:9
The lamb	Jesus, the sacrificial Lamb who atones for the world's sins	Revelation 5:5, 6; John 1:29
Babylon, the Great	A blasphemous, false religious system arrayed against God's purposes and His people	Revelation 14:8; 17:5, 6; 18:2–4
The beast	A political power that opposes God's purposes and His people	Revelation 13:1, 2, 5–7; 14:9–11; Daniel 7:7, 8, 23–25
Many waters	People groups	Revelation 17:15

A woman	God's people (His church) or a false church working against God's people	Revelation 12:1, 2; Isaiah 54:5, 6; 2 Corinthians 11:2; Revelation 17:1–6
Sodom and Egypt	A city or nation representing immorality (Sodom) and atheism (Egypt) at the end of the 1,260-day (forty-two months) prophecy	Revelation 11:8, 2; Genesis 19:4–8; Ezekiel 16:49, 50, 56–58; Exodus 5:2
Stars	Angels or demons, unless the context shows they are the literal cosmic bodies	Revelation 1:20; 9:1; 12:3, 4; 20:1–3; Job 38:4–7; Daniel 8:10
Euphrates River	People groups in support of symbolic Babylon, the false religious system. This support would eventually "dry up"	Revelation 16:11; Isaiah 44:27; 45:1; Daniel 5
Gog and Magog	The wicked in rebellion or a cipher for Babylon[2]	Revelation 20:8; Ezekiel 38:1–6
Armageddon	A final conflict over allegiance either to God the Creator or the beast and his image	Revelation 16:12–14, 16; Judges 5:19–21; 2 Corinthians 10:3–5

Principle 2: Prophetic days equal literal years

A number of major time prophecies appear in the book of Daniel such as 70 weeks, 1,260 days, 42 months, 2,300 days, and 1,335 days. Some of these are repeated in the book of Revelation. These prophecies all refer to long periods of time, and, in some cases, it is clearly stated to be so.

For example, the longest time prophecy in the Bible is the 2,300-day prophecy found in Daniel 8:14. This writer agrees with scholars who believe the prophecy began in 457 B.C.[3] If we take the 2,300 days as literal days, the prophecy would span only about six and a half years[4] and would come to its end in 451 B.C. But the Bible clearly states that "the vision refers to the time of the end" (verse 17). The angel told Daniel to "seal up the vision, for it refers to many days in the future" (verse 26).

Such a prophecy, as well as the other time prophecies in Daniel and Revelation, must be understood in terms of symbolic time. And the Bible itself gives us the clue to the meaning of these symbolic "days." God once told the prophet Ezekiel to represent the iniquity of both Israel and Judah by lying on his side a total of 430 days. Each day he lay on his side represented a literal year. God said, "I have laid on you a day for each year" (Ezekiel 4:6). God applied the same principle when He told Israel that the punishment for its unbelief at the border of Canaan would be to wander in the wilderness for forty years. "According to the number of the days in which you spied out the land, forty days, for each day you shall bear your guilt one year, namely forty years" (Numbers 14:34).

So the principle is clear. Each prophetic day should be interpreted to mean a literal year. This was so clear to the second century B.C. translators of the Septuagint (LXX), the first known translation of the Old Testament into Greek, that when they came to Daniel's seventy-week prophecy, they simply translated it as "seventy weeks of years."[5]

Below is a table highlighting the major time prophecies in apocalyptic literature, their literal time, and the time span referred to, according to standard historicist interpretation.[6]

Time Prophecy	Actual Time Length	Literal Time Span	Reference
70 weeks	490 years	From 457 B.C. to A.D. 34	Daniel 9:24; Ezra 7:7, 21, 25, 26
1,260 days, 42 months, or "time and times and half a time"[7]	1,260 years	From A.D. 538 to 1798	Daniel 7:25; 12:7; Revelation 11:2, 3; 12:6, 14; 13:5
2,300 days	2,300 years	From 457 B.C. to A.D. 1844	Daniel 8:14; Ezra 7:7, 21, 25, 26
1,335 days	1,335 years	From A.D. 508 to 1843	Daniel 12:12
1,290 days	1,290 years	From A.D. 508 to 1798	Daniel 12:11

Principle 3: Apocalyptic visions repeat and expand

This principle that apocalyptic visions repeat and expand, is sometimes known as the principle of recapitulation. It is best seen in the book of Daniel, where we find four apocalyptic visions in succession—Daniel 2; Daniel 7; Daniel 8; Daniel 9; and Daniel 10–12. The vision of Daniel 7 goes over the same subject matter given in the vision of Daniel 2, adding details and nuances not present in the first vision. In turn,

Daniel 8 and 9 expand what Daniel 7 reveals, and Daniel 10–12 gives even more minute details of the previous vision. In a similar way, the book of Revelation suggests sequences of succeeding visions that go over the same historical landscape. The vision of the seven churches (Revelation 2; 3) covers the history of the Christian church from the first century onwards. The vision of the seven seals (Revelation 6) does so in more detail. And the vision of the seven trumpets (Revelation 8; 9) does the same from a different angle—that of judgment against God's enemies.

This recapitulation does not allow for a straight-line reading of these prophecies. That is, they are not presented in chronological order, each picking up where the previous one left off. Instead, the visions are like the layers of a cake, one upon the other, describing significant developments through history. Each vision gives us more details than the one before.

Below is a table comparing the features of several prophecies and their subsequent expansions:

Prophecies of Daniel

Symbolic Meaning	Daniel 2 Symbols	Daniel 7 Symbols	Daniel 8 Symbols	Daniel 11; 12 Kings/Kingdoms[8]
Babylon	Head of gold	Lion with eagle's wings	N/A	N/A
Medo-Persia	Chest/arms of silver	Hunched bear with three ribs in his mouth	Ram with one horn higher than the other	Persian kings

Greece	Belly and thighs of bronze	Four-headed winged leopard	Male goat with one horn coming at great speed	From Alexander the Great to Antiochus IV
Imperial Rome	Legs of iron	Nondescript beast with ten horns	Little horn	Roman Caesars as kings of the North
Religious Rome	Feet of clay and iron	Little horn rising out of the ten horns	Little horn	King of the North[9]

Prophecies of John the revelator

Symbolic Meaning	Revelation 2; 3: Seven Churches	Revelation 6: Seven Seals	Revelation 8; 9: Seven Trumpets	Revelation 16: Seven Plagues
Time of Triumph	Ephesus church	Conquering white horse	Vegetation is burnt	Sores on those with the mark of the beast
Time of Tribulation	Smyrna church	Persecuting red horse	Seas become blood	The sea becomes blood; all fish die
Time of Compromise	Pergamos church	Lifeless black horse	Rivers and water springs become bitter	Rivers and water springs become blood; retribution

Time of Apostasy	Thyatira church	Deathly pale horse	The heavens become dark	The sun scorches mankind
Time of Reformation	Sardis church	Faithful saints crying for justice	Locusts torment those without the seal of God	Painful darkness torments the beast's kingdom
Time of Expansion	Philadelphia church	Second coming of Christ	Horse riders torment mankind	The Euphrates dries up, and demonic frogs appear doing miracles
Time of Ambivalence	Laodicea church	Heaven	Heaven proclaims Christ's kingdom	End of the world; Babylon receives her retribution

Principle 4: Old Testament Israel becomes the New Testament church

This is a crucial principle today. If we do not understand this principle, we will not be able to understand much of what Daniel and Revelation teach about the end times. The Bible makes it abundantly clear that the New Testament church stands for spiritual Israel, and that literal Israel is not what the apocalyptic prophecies have in mind. Let's briefly look at the evidence.[10]

When God called Abraham, His plan was to create a nation that would reveal His character and attract others to know the Him as the God of heaven. Abraham's descendants were to be a blessing to the world (Genesis 12:1–3). Israel was also to be a people of faith, that is, a people who would trust God's commandments and counsel fully. In a world in which pagan nations felt the need to appease their gods with deeds and offerings, Israel received a covenant to keep by faith in God's Word (see Exodus 19:1–8; Deuteronomy 7:6–14). "Faith was accounted to Abraham for righteousness" (Romans 4:9).

But Israel did not trust the Lord. They kept wandering after other gods until God let them do so openly, resulting in their Babylonian captivity. God gave them a second chance after they returned from their exile because, after all, they seemed to be cured from idolatry. But even though God's Word became much more precious to them, they didn't seem to get past the letter of the law (see Romans 9:30–32). Daniel's seventy-week prophecy (which we'll study in the next chapter) was God's ultimatum to Israel to respond to their Maker with transformed lives that would reflect the principles of His covenant law. From 457 b.c., they would have 490 years "to make reconciliation for iniquity" (Daniel 9:24). Instead, Israel missed the prophecies about the Servant Messiah and ended up crucifying the Lord they were supposed to proclaim.

Jesus Himself was responsible for the creation of a new Israel. In the New Testament church, He found those people who would trust His Word fully. "I say to you," He said to the Jewish leaders, "the kingdom of God will be taken from you and given to a nation bearing the fruits of it" (Matthew 21:43). And to His New Testament followers, He said, "Do not fear, little flock, for it is your Father's good pleasure to give you the kingdom" (Luke 12:32). Jesus had come to His own, but "His own did not receive Him" (John 1:11). Just days before His death, with profound pain, Jesus ratified God's severance from the nation of Israel: "O Jerusalem, Jerusalem, the one who kills the prophets and stones those who are sent to her! How often I wanted to gather your children together, as a hen gathers her chicks under her wings, but you were not willing! See! Your house [the temple] is left to you desolate" (Matthew 23:37, 38).

On the verge of the fulfillment of the seventy-week prophecy, Stephen made one last attempt to get Israel, whom he called "the congregation in the wilderness" (Acts 7:38), to reconcile with her Maker. But she would not, and instead the Jewish leaders stoned the messenger (see verses 51–58).

Later, Paul explained that in Christ, Gentiles and Jews had become one (see Ephesians 2:11–16; Galatians 3:28). Spiritual Israel had taken over the role once held by literal Israel,[11] Paul says, for "they are not all Israel who are of Israel" (Romans 9:6). The apostle explained that there is an "Israel after the flesh" (1 Corinthians 10:18), and an "Israel of God" (Galatians 6:16). The difference is no longer ethnic or cultural. The difference is spiritual. Even Israelites would now have to be "grafted in" since "because of unbelief they were broken off" (Romans 11:19, 20).

There is still time for the individual Jew to return. "If they do not continue in unbelief, [they] will be grafted in, for God is able to graft them in again" (verse 23). But this is no wholesale restoration. When Paul says "all Israel will be saved" (verse 26), he does so with the new definition of an Israelite in mind—that of the follower of Jesus, whether Jew or Gentile. That's why he reaches out to his countrymen, the Jews, that "by any means" he might "save some of them" (verse 14). Note that Paul hopes to save "some of them," not all, because he knows that not all of them will make Jesus their Savior and Lord.

People have assumed that the 1948 United Nations' resolution to establish the state of Israel is a fulfillment of Bible prophecy.[12] They forget that those biblical promises for Israel's restoration are conditional and that Israel failed miserably to meet those conditions. God told ancient Israel, "If you are unfaithful, I will scatter you among the nations; but if you return to Me . . . yet I will gather them . . . to the place which I have chosen" (Nehemiah 1:8, 9).

The first time the name *Israel* shows up in Scripture was when Jacob wrestled all night with the Angel of the Lord. Burdened with guilt and anxiety over his brother Esau's intentions for him and his family, Jacob would not let the Angel go before obtaining the assurance that his long years of deceit were forgiven and that all was right between him and God. "I will not let You go unless You bless me!" cried Jacob (Genesis 32:26). The Lord was pleased. Not only did He forgive Jacob his sins, but He immediately changed his name as a sign of the internal change that had taken place in his character. "Your name shall no longer be called Jacob, but Israel; for you have struggled with God and with men, and have prevailed" (verse 28).

Israel means "prince with God." Thus, God gave Jacob a *spiritual* name, one that identified his new character. That is the reason for Paul's teaching that those who sincerely follow Jesus are spiritual Israel. The Old Testament prophecies will be fulfilled in *them,* and not specifically in ethnic Jews.

Do not forget: Old Testament Israel becomes the New Testament church.

Do you remember the other three principles of interpreting apocalyptic prophecy? First, apocalyptic visions repeat and expand; second, prophetic days equal literal years; and third, symbols have concrete explanations. Remembering these principles that are specifically applicable to apocalyptic interpretation will help you to sort out the meaning of apocalyptic prophecies.

Now we're ready to tackle an actual apocalyptic prophecy.

CHAPTER 7

DOES DANIEL 9 TEACH ABOUT THE ANTICHRIST AND THE TRIBULATION?

The topic of the antichrist is always a hot topic of discussion. Some believe Nero, the Roman emperor who put many Christians to death in the first century, was the antichrist. Some believe it was Antiochus IV Epiphanes, the Greek king we introduced earlier in this book. However, most Christians today believe the antichrist will be an evil world leader who will rise up during the end-time Tribulation. He will enforce the mark of the beast and make, then break, a covenant with the Jews. Eventually, this antichrist will turn against Israel and devastate the Jewish temple. Although he will end up being killed, he will be resurrected during his funeral! If the *Left Behind* series is to be believed, he even has a name—Nicolae Carpathia.[1]

The big question is, Does this scenario stand up to biblical scrutiny?

In this small book, we cannot study everything about the end times, but we can tackle a key prophecy associated with the antichrist and the Tribulation that should give us some answers. That prophecy is the seventy-week prophecy found in Daniel 9:24–27. Get ready to do some careful thinking! Here is the prophecy as given in the book of Daniel:

> "Seventy weeks are determined for your people and for your holy city, to finish the transgression, to make

an end of sins, to make reconciliation for iniquity, to bring in everlasting righteousness, to seal up vision and prophecy, and to anoint the Most Holy.

"Know therefore and understand, that from the going forth of the command to restore and build Jerusalem until Messiah the Prince, there shall be seven weeks and sixty-two weeks; the street shall be built again, and the wall, even in troublesome times.

"And after the sixty-two weeks Messiah shall be cut off, but not for Himself; and the people of the prince who is to come shall destroy the city and the sanctuary. The end of it shall be with a flood, and till the end of the war desolations are determined. Then he shall confirm a covenant with many for one week; but in the middle of the week He shall bring an end to sacrifice and offering. And on the wing of abominations shall be one who makes desolate, even until the consummation, which is determined, is poured out on the desolate" (Daniel 9:24–27).

The prophecy in context

The first thing we need to do is examine the context of this prophecy. We need to allow the Bible to teach us, instead of reading into the prophecy what we, or others, think it means.

These four verses are the angel Gabriel's explanation to Daniel of part of a prophecy that had been revealed to the prophet several years earlier. In chapter 8, Daniel received a vision about a ram and a goat, representing the kingdoms of Medo-Persia and Greece (see Daniel 8:20, 21). Both rams and goats were used in the Israelite sanctuary ministry, as part of the temple sacrificial services. However, at the time of this vision, there was no temple in Jerusalem, since it had been destroyed by Nebuchadnezzar in 586 B.C.

In this vision, Daniel saw a male goat, coming "from the west" (where Greece was in relation to Medo-Persia). The goat attacked the ram "with furious power" trampling it down (Daniel 8:5, 6). This vision was fulfilled in history by the quick, effective attacks led by Alexander the Great, "the first king" of Greece (verse 21), against the Persian Empire. But even though Greece would grow "very great," at the height of its power, "the large horn [Alexander] was broken," and Alexander's kingdom was divided among "four notable ones" (verse 8), namely, his four generals.

Next Daniel saw a "little horn," the same power introduced in Daniel 7:8, who "grew exceedingly great," and cast down not just another political power, but "some of the stars [angels] to the ground," exalting himself "as high as the Prince of the host [Jesus]; and by him the daily sacrifices were taken away, and the place of His [Jesus'] sanctuary was cast down" (Daniel 8:9–11).

The question is, What does this "little horn" represent?

Many interpreters say that it represents the Seleucid king Antiochus IV Epiphanes, whom we met in a previous chapter. But there are several problems with this interpretation. First, although Antiochus did desecrate the Jewish temple, he did not cast it down, that is, destroy it. The temple itself was left intact. Second, most interpreters understand the little horn in Daniel 8 to be the same as the little horn in chapter 7. In chapter 7, the little horn rose up on the head of the fourth beast, which represents the Roman Empire. Thus, the little horn had to *follow*, or come *after*, the Roman Empire. Antiochus, on the other hand, was a Greek king, and Greece was the empire that *preceded* Rome.

A third reason for rejecting the Antiochus interpretation of the little horn in Daniel 8 is that it grew "exceedingly great" (verse 9). In other words, it was greater than both Medo-Persia and Greece that preceded it. However, Antiochus was not even the king of Greece. He was only a minor king over one of the divisions of the Greek empire. So for these reasons, and others, we must reject the Greek king Antiochus IV Epiphanes as the "little horn" in Daniel 8.

So what does this little horn represent? It symbolizes Rome in both its pagan and its religious phases. In its pagan phase, we know it as the Roman Empire. In its religious phase, it represents medieval Christianity.

Daniel said that this little horn would make a direct assault upon God's sanctuary or temple ministry. Of course, by the time medieval Christianity came on the scene, the Jewish temple had been in ruins for many centuries. Therefore, the only reasonable conclusion is that the sanctuary that is assaulted by the little horn is the sanctuary in heaven.[2] This attack was such a horrific desecration of God's ministry that Daniel heard a heavenly being, asking in despair, "How long will the vision be, concerning the daily sacrifices and the transgression of desolation, the giving of both the sanctuary and the host to be trampled underfoot?" (Daniel 8:13). In other words, "God, how long will You allow this terrible state of affairs to continue?" And the answer came, "For two thousand three hundred days; then the sanctuary shall be cleansed" (verse 14).

We've already learned that in time prophecies a day equals a year (see Ezekiel 6:4; Numbers 14:34). So, the period mentioned here is 2,300 years, something Gabriel ratified by telling Daniel, "Understand, son of man, that the vision refers to the time of the end" (Daniel 8:17). Daniel understood that this desecration of God's ministry in the heavenly sanctuary would continue for over two thousand years, and he "fainted and was sick for days," and he "was astonished by the vision, but no one understood it" (verse 27).

Gabriel comes back with the explanation

Years went by, during which time Daniel "went about the king's business" (verse 27). He couldn't make a lot of sense of the 2,300-day (year) prophecy, even though Gabriel had tried to explain it to him (see verses 19–26), because he fainted just as the angel had started to explain the meaning of this time period.

However, when the predicted seventy years of the Babylonian captivity were about finished, Daniel set out to intercede by prayer on behalf of his people Israel (see Daniel 9:1–3). He pleaded with God, "Let Your anger and Your fury be turned away from Your city Jerusalem . . . Cause Your face to shine on Your sanctuary, which is desolate" (verses 16, 17). "Oh Lord," Daniel prayed. "Do not delay for Your own sake . . . for Your city and Your people are called by Your name" (verse 19).

In other words, Daniel prayed that God would allow the Jews to return to Jerusalem and restore their city and temple. His concern for God's people and the sanctuary is what links his prayer with the vision of Daniel 8, where the little horn power oppresses God's people and desecrates the sanctuary ministry.

Quite unexpectedly, while Daniel was still praying for an understanding of the fate of his people, their city, and their sanctuary, he received another visit from the angel Gabriel, who had tried to explain "the vision at the beginning" (verse 21), that is, the vision of chapter 8 concerning the little horn and its attack on God's sanctuary ministry.

Gabriel told the prophet, "O Daniel, I have now come forth to give you skill to understand. . . . Therefore, consider the matter, and understand the vision" (verses 22, 23). The word for "vision" in this verse is the Hebrew word *mareh,* which refers to the specific vision of the 2,300 days Daniel had seen earlier. So, Gabriel now would satisfy both of Daniel's needs. He would answer the prophet's concern for the Jews and Jerusalem, and he would also explain the visions of the 2,300 days (years) given to him in chapter 8.

Seventy weeks determined for Israel

Now that we have established the historical and linguistic context of the seventy-week prophecy, we can figure out its meaning. Gabriel begins by saying that "seventy weeks are determined for your people and for your holy city" (verse 24). The word *determined* is the Hebrew word *hatak,* which means, literally, "cut off." Cut off from what? Cut off from the longer 2,300-year prophecy. And since 70 weeks equal 490 days, these 490 prophetic *days* equal 490 literal *years.* So, evidently, Gabriel is going to explain the meaning of the first 490 years of the entire 2,300 years of the prophecy.

Among other things, the seventy-week prophecy predicts the time when Jesus, the Messiah, would be on earth. Gabriel called Him "Messiah the Prince" (verse 25). The Hebrew word *mesiach* transliterated into English as "Messiah," means "Anointed One." According to the apostle Peter, Jesus became the Anointed One, the Messiah, at the time of His baptism at the Jordan (see Acts 10:37, 38). And we know that Jesus was "about thirty years of age" (Luke 3:23) when He was baptized "in the fifteenth year of the reign of Tiberius Caesar" (verse 1). Since we have historical records that can determine which year was the fifteenth year of Tiberius, we subtract thirty years and arrive at the year of Jesus' birth. The best calculations point to the year 4 or 5 B.C.

Gabriel said these 490 years were determined, or cut off, for Israel and Jerusalem. In what way? The answer comes in six poetic phrases. The first two describe what God's people were to accomplish by the time the Messiah came. They were "to finish the transgression," and "to make an end of sins" (Daniel 9:24). The Hebrew word translated as "transgression" is *peshah,* which means rebellion against God Himself. So, they were to finish their "rebellion." For centuries, Israel had been idolatrous like the nations surrounding it. But God was now giving His people 490 years of probation to see if they would finally stop this rebellion against Him and make an end of their sins.

The next two poetic phrases describe what God would do. The Messiah would "make reconciliation for iniquity" and "bring in everlasting righteousness" (verse 24). This could not be accomplished by Israel. Many Bible versions translate this phrase as "atonement," rather than "reconciliation,"[3] because the Hebrew word used here is *kipper,* which means "atonement." Only the Messiah could atone for iniquity, and everlasting righteousness could only be the result of Christ's victory over evil at the cross.

The last two phrases point to the results of the work of the Messiah and the work of His people: "to seal up vision and prophecy, and to anoint the Most Holy" (verse 24). This is a little more complex. It speaks of what would happen when the time of this prophecy was fulfilled. We'll explain these phrases when we have established the time of the prophecy's fulfillment.

The timing of the prophecy

Gabriel gave Daniel (and us) the time for the beginning of the prophecy—the time when the 2,300 days (years) were to commence. Here is what he said, "Know therefore and understand, that from the going forth of the command to restore and build Jerusalem until Messiah the Prince, there shall be seven weeks and sixty-two weeks" (verse 25). So the prophecy begins when the command goes forth to restore and rebuild Jerusalem. The books of Ezra and Nehemiah refer to four decrees by Medo-Persian kings dealing with the return of the exiles and the rebuilding of Jerusalem and the temple. One of them should be the command Gabriel is speaking of.

The first decree was made in 537 B.C. by Cyrus. It was an order to rebuild the temple (see Ezra 1:1–4; 6:3–5; 2 Chronicles 36:22, 23). Nothing was said in this decree about rebuilding the city. The second was issued by Darius (see Ezra 6:1–12) in 519 B.C. It basically reaffirmed Cyrus's earlier decree to rebuild the temple. The work on the temple was then resumed.

The fourth decree was issued by Artaxerxes I to Nehemiah in 444 B.C. (see Nehemiah 2:1), although it can scarcely be called a decree. It is more of a letter of safe passage and support for Nehemiah to rebuild the city's walls. However, some scholars consider this to be the decree in question, and thus start the seventy-week prophecy in the year 444 B.C. But Nehemiah didn't rebuild Jerusalem; he only worked on the walls and the gates, completing the entire job in only fifty-two days (see Nehemiah 6:15). This means that most of the rebuilding work would have already been completed.

The major rebuilding of Jerusalem took place in the time of Ezra (see Ezra 4:7–23; 9:25), since those opposed to the task were complaining about the rebuilding of the city and the repair of its foundations (see Ezra 4:12). This work was undertaken by authority of the "third decree," which was an extension of the main decree to rebuild the city. It is the only one that can apply (see Ezra 7:7, 8) and was issued by Artaxerxes I in the year 457 B.C.[4]

From here onward, following the timeline of the prophecy is simple math. Gabriel said that "from the going forth of the command to restore and to build Jerusalem" would be "seven weeks and sixty-two weeks," (Daniel 9:25) for a total of sixty-nine prophetic weeks, which is 483 literal years. During this time, the Jews would have to demonstrate their faithfulness to God and His covenant. If we subtract 483 years from 457 B.C., we are left with twenty-six years that extend into A.D. time. However, since there is no "year zero" between B.C. and A.D. time, we have to add a year to the A.D. date, making the year for the appearance of the Messiah A.D. 27. *And that is the exact year when Jesus was baptized!* This is exciting, because we realize that God predicted the exact year when Jesus would be baptized, that is, anointed, for His ministry.

And since the 490 years were to be "cut off" from the longer 2,300 days (years), we can now calculate the end of the 2,300 days or years. The 2,300 years will obviously have to extend into A.D. time, and when we subtract 457 B.C. from 2,300 we come up with the year 1843. However, we must add a year to the A.D. date (remember, there is no "year zero" between B.C. and A.D. time), and this brings us to 1844 as the ending date for the 2,300-day prophecy. The year 1844 isn't really that long ago.

Unfortunately, some Christians today arbitrarily split off the final week of the seventy-week prophecy from the rest of the 490 years and push it down to the time of the end. There is absolutely no scriptural basis to suggest such a split. This is sometimes referred to as the gap theory, because it creates a huge gap of thousands of years between the sixty-nine prophetic weeks and the final week of Daniel's prophecy.

The Prince and His people

The angel Gabriel goes on to say that "after the sixty-two weeks Messiah shall be cut off, but not for Himself" (verse 26). That is, during the last week, between the years A.D. 27 and 34, Jesus would be "cut off." This expression is an idiom referring to the Messiah's death, and since the verb is used in the passive (*Niphal*) conjugation, it means that someone else would cause His death. That is, He would not die a natural death. And Christ clearly did not die for Himself nor did He commit suicide, and no one was there for Him either.

The following verse amplifies this situation. "Then he shall confirm a covenant with many for one week; but in the middle of the week He shall bring an end to sacrifice and offering" (verse 27). The end to "sacrifice and offering" would come "in the middle of the week," that is, the middle between the year A.D. 27 and 34. This happened at the Cross, three and a half years into His ministry.

How did the Messiah do that? Well, the Bible tells us Jesus is the Lamb of God who takes away the sin of the world (see John 1:29). He is the Antitype, the fulfillment, of all the sanctuary ministry types. He is the ultimate Sacrifice. All the Old Testament sacrifices were only "a shadow of things to come" (Colossians 2:17). When Jesus came, and died on Calvary, the need for sacrifices and offering became irrelevant (see Hebrews 9:11–15). Jesus was, and is, the ultimate Sacrifice to which all the other Old Testament sacrifices point. Even though the Jews kept offering sacrifices in Jerusalem after the Crucifixion, God Himself had confirmed that these sacrifices were no longer relevant by tearing the veil separating the Holy Place from the Most Holy Place in the temple from top to bottom the moment Jesus died (see Matthew 27:50, 51).

Gabriel also said, "He shall confirm a covenant with many

for one week" (Daniel 9:27). Here, "he" has to refer to Messiah the Prince, Jesus. He is *confirming* a covenant that had already been made. God's original covenant with Israel was the Ten Commandment covenant made at Mount Sinai (see Exodus 19:4–7; 34:28). When Jesus expounded on the commandments in His famous sermon on the mount, He was confirming to His listeners the fact that He was not doing away with any part of it. In fact, Jesus said, "Till heaven and earth pass away, one jot or one tittle will by no means pass from the law till all is fulfilled," and "unless your righteousness exceeds the righteousness of the scribes and Pharisees, you will be no means enter the kingdom of heaven" (Matthew 5:18, 20). He confirmed the covenant for the last prophetic week—the last seven years—the first half of which were fulfilled His ministry. The second half were the three and a half years of the New Testament church, ending with the stoning of Stephen. Stephen was God's last messenger to the Jews (see Acts 7). When the Jews stoned the last prophet of the covenant in A.D. 34, Israel's time of probation, the 490 years, expired.

But let's go back to Daniel 9:26 for a moment. The second part of that verse confuses some people, because it sounds like it is referring to somebody other than the Messiah. The text reads, "And the people of the prince who is to come shall destroy the city and the sanctuary. The end of it shall be with a flood, and till the end of the war desolations are determined" (verse 26). The problem arises if we assume that "the prince" in this verse is not the same individual as the "Prince" in verse 25. We already pointed out that the Hebrew language does not use capitalization, so the fact that in English Bibles "the Prince" is capitalized in verse 25, but not in verse 26 does not mean that the verses are referring to two different individuals.

There is no such distinction in Hebrew. In fact, logic dictates that since "the Prince" in verse 25 is clearly identified as the Messiah, "the prince" in verse 26 should also be the Messiah.

What mystifies some Bible students is why the people of the Messiah would destroy Jerusalem, their own city! This destruction took place in A.D. 70. We already heard the story in chapter 2. The Jews were responsible for the destruction of Jerusalem by their stubborn resistance to the Roman siege and by using the temple as a fortress. Titus, the Roman general, was not at all interested in burning the temple or destroying the city. He just wanted militant Jews to surrender. So even though, technically, Jerusalem was destroyed by the Romans, those ultimately responsible for its destruction were the Jews, the people of Messiah the Prince.

There is a precedence for this. Six hundred years earlier, when the Babylonians besieged Jerusalem, King Zedekiah of Judah went against every counsel given by God's prophets and resisted the Babylonians. Nebuchadnezzar ended up burning the city. But it was King Zedekiah who was to blame for the city's destruction.

In A.D. 70, the Romans burned most of the city and tore down its walls. When Emperor Hadrian visited the site sixty years later, "he found the temple of God trodden down and the whole city devastated save for a few houses."[5] The desolations determined until the end of the war (see Daniel 9:26) were clearly fulfilled in A.D. 70.

Where is the antichrist?

The last sentence in the prophecy ties the 490 years with the rest of the 2,300 years, the longer portion of the prophecy. "And on the wing of abominations shall be one who makes desolate, even until the consummation, which is determined, is poured out on the desolate" (verse 27).

The references to "desolation" in this prophecy have to do with the destruction of Jerusalem, less than forty years after the time that Israel's probation expired. The ending of the sacrifices and offering had nothing to do with any antichrist; it was Christ who brought the Jewish temple services to an end when He had died as God's Lamb on the cross. In doing this, He made Israel's sacrifices null and void from that time forward.

The seven years, the last prophetic week, are not separate from the rest of the prophecy. There is no gap theory in the Bible. It simply defies all logic to split the seventy-week prophecy into two parts when nothing in Daniel's prophecy suggests doing this. But even more to the point, those seven years have nothing to do with a tribulation period. The "seven-year tribulation" is simply an invention of John Darby, which he needed in order to justify bringing the Jews back to Jesus at the time of the end.

The last seven years of the seventy-week prophecy is the time of the confirmation of the covenant God made with the Jews, the last seven years of their probation. Because they failed to be faithful to God and accept His Messiah, the Jews, as a nation, ran out of time. The church is now composed of individual Jews and Gentiles, who have chosen to follow the Master. God's people are no longer limited to one ethnic group.

That there will be a Tribulation at the end of time is clear from Daniel 12, but not from Daniel 9. In Daniel 12, God told Daniel, "At that time Michael shall stand up, the great prince who stands watch over the sons of your people; and there shall be a time of trouble, such as never was since there was a nation" (verse 1). That Tribulation *does* come at the end of time. But the Bible says nothing about the rebuilding of the *temple* at the end of time. The references to temple building all have to do with the second temple, Herod's temple, destroyed in A.D. 70.

It is easy to read into a text what one has already decided it should say. But a careful reading of the text, keeping in mind context and language, will bring out the truth that God desires to share with His people.

And when you know the truth, "the truth shall make you free" (John 8:32).

CHAPTER 8
WORSHIP: THE BIG ISSUE IN REVELATION

In the book of Revelation we find the great struggle of the ages between good and evil. This is clearly seen in some of the symbols used in the book: the Lamb (Revelation 5) versus the dragon (Revelation 12); the pure woman (Revelation 12) versus the scarlet whore (Revelation 17); the seal of God (Revelation 7) versus the mark of the beast (Revelation 13).

In this conflict between Christ and Satan, there is a single issue that rises to the top: *Whom shall we worship?* It would seem that the entire book of Revelation is focused on this topic. The following table gives a few examples showing how pervasive the subject is in the book of Revelation, contrasting the worship of God with the worship of demons:

Text	Worshiping God	Worshiping the Enemy
Revelation 1:5, 6, 17	John reacts with exaltation and humility as he thinks of/sees Jesus	
Revelation 4:8–11	Heavenly beings worship God "day and night"	

Revelation 9:20, 21		Mankind who do not heed God's sixth trumpet warning still worship demons
Revelation 11:1	God's faithful people are seen worshiping in God's temple	
Revelation 13:8, 12		The whole world worships the beast
Revelation 14:7	The first angel's message calls for mankind to worship the Creator	
Revelation 14:9–11		The third angel's message warns about the destructive aftermath of worshiping the beast and his image
Revelation 15:4	All nations worship God once they see His righteous judgments	
Revelation 19:10; 22:8, 9	John is told to worship God and not the angel	

Why worship?

The Bible makes it very clear that the object of our worship should be the God of heaven. And it also makes plain the reason why we should worship Him: He is the Creator; He made us. Here is the way the psalmist expresses it:

O come, let us sing to the LORD!
Let us shout joyfully to the Rock of our salvation.
Let us come before His presence with thanksgiving;
Let us shout joyfully to Him with psalms.
For the LORD is the great God,
And the great King above all gods.
In His hand are the deep places of the earth;
The height of the hills are His also.
The sea is His, for He made it;
And His hands formed the dry land.
O come, let us worship and bow down;
Let us kneel before the LORD our Maker.
For He is our God,
And we are the people of His pasture,
And the sheep of His hand (Psalm 95:1–7).

The English word *worship* originated from the Anglo-Saxon word *weorthscipe,* or "worth-ship," meaning "someone worthy of honor and reverence." When we worship God, we believe in His worthiness.[1] He has the right to our worship, because He created us, and without Him we simply would not exist. "You are worthy, O Lord," cried the twenty-four elders in the throne room of heaven, "to receive glory and honor and power; for You created all things, and by Your will they exist and were created" (Revelation 4:11).

The New Testament word most often translated as "worship" is the Greek word *proskuneo,* which means, literally, "to kiss the hand toward one." Do you see the picture? It is as if royalty appears, extending his hand for you to kiss. You prostrate yourself, you bow in reverence before the person who graces the room.[2]

Creation, however, is not the only reason we should worship God. We also worship Him because of His redemptive work on our behalf, because of His salvation! This is why, although expressions of worship in Revelation 4 focus on God's creative power, those in Revelation 5 focus on His sacrifice for sinners: "Worthy is the Lamb who was slain to receive power and riches and wisdom, and strength and honor and glory and blessing!" (Revelation 5:12). Notice that the focus on creation elicits three statements of praise: glory, honor, and power (see Revelation 4:11); but the focus on His work of redemption draws seven statements of praise: power, riches, wisdom, strength, honor, glory, and blessing. And we have learned that seven is the number symbolic of completion or perfection. Redemption completed God's work on behalf of mankind.

Both of these reasons—creation and redemption—were already hinted at in the Old Testament. For example, a number of chapters in Isaiah, one after the other, bring out these points clearly. "I have made the earth, and created man on it. I—My hands—stretched out the heavens, and all their host I have commanded" (Isaiah 45:12). Let's pause for a moment. This is what I like to call *God's signature,* the unique way in which He identifies Himself as God. His creative power covers three areas: He created the heavens (the universe), the earth, and mankind on it. This same formula is repeated a number of times (see Isaiah 42:5; 44:24; 45:18; 51:13, 16). "Tell and bring forth your case," God continues to say through Isaiah. "Yes, let them take counsel together. Who has declared this from ancient time? Who has told it from that time? Have not I, the Lord? And there is no other God besides Me, a just God and a Savior; there is none besides Me. Look to Me, and be saved, all you ends of the earth! For I am God, and there is no other" (Isaiah 45:21, 22).

We human beings owe everything to God because He not

only made us to begin with, He purchased us back to remake us in newness of life!

The heart of Revelation

This double emphasis of creation and redemption as the reason for our worship appears to shift when we get closer to the heart of Revelation.

In chapter 5, we looked at the structure of Revelation, and you'll recall that the most important part of the book is in the middle, not at the end. This is the "great conflict" section, Revelation 10 through 14. In this section, we find the opening of the little book (Revelation 10), the rise and demise of the two witnesses (Revelation 11), the persecution and deliverance of the church (Revelation 12), the persecution of the saints by the beast and its image (Revelation 13), the characteristics of the 144,000, the last three messages God has for all the world, and the coming of Christ (Revelation 14).

At the start of this middle section, John sees a mighty angel "standing on the sea and on the land" who "swore by Him who lives forever and ever, who created heaven and the things that are in it, the earth and the things that are in it, and the sea and the things that are in it, that there should be delay no longer" (Revelation 10:5, 6).

What does "delay no longer" mean? A literal translation would read, "time will be no more." This does not mean the end of history, but the end of time prophecies. The Greek word for "time" is *chronos,* that is, measured time to finish "the mystery of God" (verse 7). And all this is in the context of a little book that is now open (see verse 8). The one biblical reference to an open book that was closed was the book of Daniel, when God told him to "seal the book until the time of the end" (Daniel 12:4). In other words, Revelation 10 is saying that the time prophecies of Daniel have now come to an end. That book is now open.[3]

But the point we should not miss is the context of this end-of-time pronouncement. The context is *creation*. The angel's declaration that prophetic time has expired is given on the basis of a God who created heaven and earth (see Revelation 10:6)! This is intriguing, because at the end of the center portion of Revelation, we find another major declaration also made on the basis of God's creation. This time, the focus is on worship, the issue at the heart of the heart of the book of Revelation:

> Then I saw another angel flying in the midst of heaven, having the everlasting gospel to preach to those who dwell on the earth—to every nation, tribe, tongue, and people—saying with a loud voice, "Fear God and give glory to Him, for the hour of His judgment has come; and worship Him who made heaven and earth, the sea and springs of water" (Revelation 14:6, 7).

Again, the reason that this passage gives for worship goes back to the beginning—to creation. For some reason, at the time of the end, when "there should be delay no longer," people will have forgotten from whom they came, whose handiwork they really are. And God is calling out with a loud voice for His followers to remember that He is their Maker.

Evolutionary worldviews and secular trends in daily living have influenced people to forget their Creator God. But God is calling us back to basics. The summons by the first angel to worship the Creator (see Revelation 14:7) is in contrast with the third angel's message:

Then a third angel followed them, saying with a loud voice, "If anyone worships the beast and his image, and receives his mark on his forehead or on his hand, he himself shall also drink of the wine of the wrath of God, which is poured out full strength into the cup of His indignation" (verses 9, 10).

This warning refers to the previous chapter (Revelation 13) where we're told that people "worshiped the dragon who gave authority to the beast; and they worshiped the beast" because "the image of the beast" had the power to cause "all, both small and great, rich and poor, free and slave, to receive a mark on their right hand or on their foreheads," so that "no one may buy or sell except" those with "the mark" (verses 4, 15–17).

The heart of the book of Revelation is telling us that worship will be a matter of life or death at the end. Those who worship the beast will incur God's wrath, and those who don't won't be able to buy or sell. It will all boil down to our loyalty, to whatever we consider worth our allegiance to the point that we would stake our lives on it. Will we be inclined to risk our lives in order to worship the Creator God? In the end, there will be only two kinds of people: those who worship the beast, and those who worship God the Creator.

The devil in the details

This emphasis on creation reminds us of why evil began in the first place. According to the book of Ezekiel, Lucifer was a perfect, righteous angel "on the holy mountain of God" (God's throne), until "iniquity was found" in him (Ezekiel 28:14, 15). Something happened with Lucifer. One reason, the Bible gives, is that he began to pay attention to his "beauty" and "splendor" (verse 17). Isaiah expands on this: "How you are fallen from heaven, O Lucifer, son of the morning! . . . For you have said in your heart: 'I will ascend into heaven, I will exalt my throne above the stars [angels] of God; . . . I will ascend above the heights of the clouds, I will be like the Most High' " (Isaiah 14:12–14). Lucifer wanted to share the Godhead's privileges. No longer content to be a mere angel, he thought himself entitled to homage akin to God's because he was such a magnificent being. Lucifer sought worship just like God received it from the angels (see Hebrews 1:6).

When Lucifer—now Satan—confronted Jesus in the wilderness, he couldn't help revealing his craving for worship. After all, he was the prince of this world! Exhibiting remarkable impertinence, the prince of darkness said to Jesus, the Creator, " 'All these things [the kingdoms of the world] I will give You if You will fall down and worship me.' Then Jesus said to him, 'Away with you, Satan! For it is written, "You shall worship the LORD your God, and Him only you shall serve" ' " (Matthew 4:9, 10). Lucifer was a created being. He was not God.

The memorial of Creation

Creation reminds us that we are not God and that He is worthy of all our adoration and worship. And to help us remember Him as the Creator, God gave us the Sabbath as a memorial of His creation. "Remember the Sabbath day," God said, "to keep it holy. Six days you shall labor and do all your work, but the seventh day is the Sabbath of the LORD your God" (Exodus 20:8–10). And why was Israel to keep the Sabbath? God's fourth commandment also gave the answer: "For in six days the LORD made the heavens and the earth, the sea, and all that is in them, and rested the seventh day. Therefore the LORD blessed the Sabbath day and hallowed it [made it holy]" (verse 11).

Some believe this Sabbath commandment applied only to the Jews, but it cannot be so. If it were, the first or the fifth or the seventh commandment should also be only for the Jews. Scripture makes it clear that God's commandments are eternal (see John 12:50) and that they are for everyone (see Revelation 22:14).[4] Besides, the commandment itself harks back to Creation (see Genesis 2:1–3), which took place two thousand years before Abraham, the first Jew, walked on the earth.

Others believe that Jesus' death and resurrection made the seventh-day Sabbath obsolete.[5] But neither Christ nor the Bible ever said so. The weight of evidence in the New Testament is that the apostles kept teaching and keeping the seventh-day Sabbath just like their Master had done (see Acts 13:42, 44; Hebrews 4:4, 9–11; Luke 4:16).[6]

Sincere Christians sometimes argue that any day of the week in which we honor God is good enough. But God's commandment is very explicit: we have six days to do our business, while the seventh day is the time that belongs to God. When the Pharisees argued in favor of their own ideas in lieu of God's, Jesus responded, "In vain they worship Me, teaching as doctrines the commandments of men" (Mark 7:7). Even John the revelator opposed this kind of thinking. In one of his letters, he wrote, "Now by this we know that we know Him, if we keep His commandments. He who says, 'I know Him,' and does not keep His commandments, is a liar, and the truth is not in him" (1 John 2:3, 4). The Sabbath commandment is one of God's Ten Commandments and is as binding and as important as the other nine.

If someone is to blame for the change of the Sabbath—the day that God clearly said to "remember,"—it would be the "little horn" power. The prophecy says that he would "speak pompous words against the Most High, shall persecute the saints of the Most High, *and shall intend to change times and law*" (Daniel 7:25; emphasis supplied). Since his activity is "against the Most High" it must be God's law that the "little horn" power is trying to change, and the one commandment of God's law that deals with time is the fourth commandment—the one about the Sabbath.

This passage in Daniel was written in Aramaic. In Aramaic, a span of time, such as the prophetic 1,260 days, is identified by the word *iddan,* whereas a point of time is expressed by the word *zimmin.* Daniel 7:25 uses the word *zeman,* the plural of *zimmin,* which means specific, repeated points of time. In other words, the little horn intends to change a specific time in the law of God, in contrast with a span of time, like the time of Tribulation—and the only point of time mentioned in the Ten Commandments, specifically and repeatedly, is the seventh-day Sabbath (see Exodus 20:8–11).[7]

Implications for last-day people

The implications are profound for anyone wanting to take God seriously. The Sabbath reflects a much greater reality than a mere twenty-four-hour period. It puts the spotlight on God as the subject and the object of our worship. "God is the primary subject of the seventh day," someone wrote recently. "When we speak of the lost meaning of the seventh day, therefore, we are speaking of meaning that has been lost concerning God. The seventh day draws attention to a subject more important than itself."[8]

The Sabbath is much more than just a day in the week. It is the day of God, "a sanctuary in time"[9] which the Son of God created in order to commune with His creation. It is "a sign between" God and us so we may know that God is "the LORD who sanctifies" us (Ezekiel 20:12). The seventh-day, or the Bible's, Sabbath is like a telescope allowing us a closer glimpse of the eternal God who made us for His glory.

No substitutes will do. Take, for instance, the United States flag. It is very specific and easy to identify among the flags of the family of nations: thirteen horizontal red and white stripes with fifty white stars on a rectangular patch of blue. Why can't a flag with a green stripe or with the sun in the middle stand for our country? Because the flag is a symbol of a very concrete underlying reality. "It participates in the power and dignity of the nation for which it stands."[10] The only time you can do away with the flag is when the country it represents is done away with.

The Sabbath is God's token of Creation. It uniquely points to God, because during six days He created the world and its teeming creatures, but on the seventh day He created time. The Sabbath is the day God blessed and made holy (see Genesis 2:1–3). The first thing God consecrated in this world was not a thing nor a place, but a moment in time. And this speaks of the powerful relationship God seeks to establish with human beings. Everyone knows that if you want to demonstrate real love and care for another, gifts, toys, and chocolates will go only so far. The real test of love is whether or not you are is willing to spend your *time* with someone else. This is what God demonstrated at Creation. God made time and chose to spend that time with us.

The question is, Will we reciprocate?

"He who has My commandments and keeps them," Jesus said, "it is he who loves Me. And he who loves Me will be loved by My Father, and I will love him and manifest Myself to him" (John 14:21).

The Lord is still calling out, "Remember the Sabbath day, to keep it holy" (Exodus 20:8). We live in the time of the end.

The door of opportunity to respond in faith to God is open now. Will you be His alone?

CHAPTER 9

CAN WE EXPECT PROPHETS AT THE TIME OF THE END?

When Jesus started His public ministry, He erupted on the scene with a prophetic message: "The time is fulfilled, and the kingdom of God is at hand. Repent, and believe in the gospel" (Mark 1:15; cf. Matthew 4:17), that is, "the good news" (NIV). Jesus' message had three components: (1) a specific time prophecy had now been fulfilled, (2) the kingdom of God was present, and (3) repentance and belief in the gospel are now necessary, because of the first two components.

When John the Baptist proclaimed the same message in the Judean desert, "Repent, for the kingdom of heaven is at hand" (Matthew 3:2), he did not include the first part—the part about the time being fulfilled—because Jesus, the Messiah, hadn't quite yet appeared to begin His ministry. The prophets had foretold that the Messiah would come, and He did come—exactly on time (see Galatians 4:4). As soon as Jesus was baptized in the Jordan to begin His public ministry, the time prophecy of Daniel 9:25 was fulfilled. He was anointed the Messiah (see Acts 10:38), the Prince of Daniel's prophecy.

John the Baptist was a man "filled with the Holy Spirit, even from his mother's womb" (Luke 1:15). His ministry was critical to the work of Christ, to "turn many of the children of Israel to the Lord" (verse 16). He was "the voice of one crying in the wilderness: 'Prepare the way of the LORD; make His paths straight' " (Luke 3:4). His message was one of repentance and reform (see Matthew 3:8–11; Mark 1:4; Luke 3:1–3).

The work of John the Baptist to prepare people to receive the Messiah makes us ponder about how and when God uses prophets. As mentioned earlier, the role of the prophet is two-fold: to foretell the future and to tell forth God's will. It seems that in the past, for every major event affecting His people, God used a predicting prophet as well as an equipping one. One or more prophets would first forecast a major event to come, and then, as the time for the fulfillment of the prophecy drew near, often hundreds of years later, God would raise up one or more prophets to prepare or equip His people for what was about to take place in the fulfillment of the prophecy. This distinction does not mean that a given prophet *only* either predicted or prepared. Most did both throughout their ministries. But the timing of their service to God, as well as their unique roles, determined their focus—either on predicting or preparing.

Here is a chart showing a few of the major events in the history of God's people and the predictive and equipping prophets God used for each occasion.

Event	Predicting Prophets	Equipping Prophets
The Flood	*Enoch* (via Methuselah)[1] Genesis 5:21–27	*Noah* Genesis 6:3, 4, 6–8
The Exodus	*Abraham* Genesis 15:13, 14	*Moses* Exodus 3:6–10; Acts 7:17, 20, 32–34

The Exile	*Moses, Ahijah* Deuteronomy 28:49–68; 1 Kings 14:15, 16	*Jeremiah* Jeremiah 25:1–11
The Messiah: Christ's First Coming	*Daniel, Isaiah* Daniel 9:25; Isaiah 40:3, 4	*John the Baptist* John 1:14, 15, 19–23
The Second Coming of Jesus	*Peter, Paul, James, etc.* 1 Peter 3:9–13; 1 Thessalonians 5:1–3; James 5:7, 8	?

You probably noticed one empty section left blank except for a question mark. The second coming of Christ is the next major event in the history of God's people. Since God's use of predicting and equipping prophets seems so consistent throughout the past, should we not expect a prophet or prophets that would prepare God's people for the return of Jesus?

The time of the end

In Scripture, the expression "the time of the end," is very explicit, and it appears only in the prophecies of Daniel. Daniel 8 presents the longest time prophecy in the Bible: " 'How long will the vision be, concerning the daily sacrifices and the transgression of desolation, the giving of both the sanctuary and the host to be trampled under foot?' And he said to me, 'For two thousand three hundred days; then the sanctuary shall be cleansed' " (Daniel 8:13, 14).

We have already learned that a prophetic day equals a literal year (see Numbers 14:34). Thus the 2,300 days are actual years. We also learned from our study of Daniel 9 that this prophecy begins in 457 B.C. Subtracting the 457 B.C. date from

2,300 years leads us to the year A.D. 1844. Since there was no sanctuary on earth in 1844 that could possibly fulfill the prophecy, it must refer to the sanctuary in heaven that will be cleansed. Something very significant must have taken place in heaven in 1844, but we will have to leave the explanation of this aspect of the prophecy for another time. Right now we want to focus on the fact that only three verses further, the angel Gabriel pinpointed "the time of the end," by saying to Daniel, "understand, son of man, that the vision refers to the time of the end" (verse 17). Thus, wherever the book of Daniel mentions "the time of the end" (see, for example, Daniel 11:35, 40; 12:4, 9), it refers to this same period beginning in A.D. 1844, less than two hundred years ago.

The last two times this expression—"the time of the end"—is used it is in connection with the sealing, or closing, of the book of Daniel (see Daniel 12:4, 9). The book was to be closed until "the time of the end" when "many shall run to and fro, and knowledge" of the book "shall increase" (Daniel 12:4). Not surprisingly, we find in Revelation—Daniel's companion prophetic book—the mention of a little book open when "there should be time no longer" (Revelation 10:6, KJV), when "the mystery of God would be finished" (verse 7). In other words, there would be no more prophetic time after 1844. All the time prophecies would have come to an end by that time.

What event in history corresponds with the fulfillment of these prophecies? History records a movement in New England led by an individual named William Miller, a Baptist farmer in upstate New York. Miller's movement paralleled a number of revivals breaking out all over the world, because of their focus on prophecy and the coming of the Lord.[2]

After his conversion from deism, Miller set out to study the

Bible, chapter by chapter. In 1818, after two years of this daily Bible study routine, he came across the 2,300-day prophecy in the book of Daniel and assumed the cleansing of the sanctuary predicted there meant the cleansing of the earth by fire (see 2 Peter 3:12). In Miller's mind, this could encompass nothing less than the end of the world and the coming of Christ. Not entirely sure of his interpretation, however, it took Miller another thirteen years before he shared his views with others. But when he did, the study of the book of Daniel took off like wildfire on dry grass.

Soon, ministers of Congregational, Presbyterian, Methodist, and various other denominational churches joined Miller in preaching the prophecies of Daniel and the soon coming of Christ. Not realizing that there is a sanctuary in heaven to be cleansed, their attention was focused on the cleansing of the earth, causing them to expect the literal coming of Jesus in the clouds very soon.

The Millerite movement, in spite of scorn by unbelievers, had powerful positive effects. Tens of thousands focused on Jesus, surrendering their all to Him, and while looking forward to His coming, they shared the good news with everyone they knew. Miller and his followers eventually determined that the prophecy was to be fulfilled on October 22, 1844, the day on which the Jewish Day of Atonement (Yom Kippur) fell in that particular year. The Day of Atonement was the annual festival commemorating Israel's annual cleansing of the Old Testament sanctuary.

But Jesus did not return on the expected date. He did not return, because the prophecy was not about His coming. After all, He Himself had said of His return: "Of that day and hour no one knows, not even the angels of heaven" (Matthew 24:36). Instead, the prophecy was about the cleansing of God's sanctuary in heaven.[3]

It was clear to all who were involved in those days in Miller's movement that the Spirit of God had been mightily poured upon many, not only in New England, but around the world as well. Even if they did not yet understand what took place in heaven, they clearly sensed something significant had taken place on earth.

In retrospect, it is easy to see that "the time of the end" *began* in 1844—more than 160 years ago. That may seem like a long time to us, but from the perspective of the entire history of the world, and of God in particular, this is a relatively short time.

More than a prophet

At this time in its history, the church of God should expect an equipping prophet to "prepare the way of the LORD" (Matthew 3:3). Just as John the Baptist was the equipping prophet for the first coming of Christ, God would surely have someone to prepare His people for Jesus' second coming.

This is particularly so, because John was "more than a prophet" (Matthew 11:9). What did John do to deserve such an honor? He was full of the Spirit of God (see Luke 1:15, 80). He preached repentance and reformation (see Mark 1:4; Luke 3:4–8). He constantly lifted up Jesus before the people (see John 1:15–18, 29). He gave practical counsel on how to live the life of faith daily (Luke 3:10–14). He exemplified a simple, healthy lifestyle (see Mark 1:6; Matthew 11:18). He fearlessly confronted those in sin (see Matthew 14:3, 4). He spent much time with God (see Luke 1:80). He didn't perform miracles, but spoke the truth (see John 10:40–42). People sensed that he was on the same spiritual level as some of the greatest prophets of old (see Luke 9:7, 8). But the chief reason John was "more than a prophet" was his role in history. He was God's instrument to prepare people for the coming of the Messiah (see Luke 1:68–79).

In these last days, God's church should expect someone who is "more than a prophet," even if that person will never be included in the canon of Scripture. (The Bible mentions a number of prophets whose writings were not included in the canon.[4]) Therefore, we should expect God to send someone who not only can anticipate things about the future, but who can prepare us for them. Someone who is full of the Spirit, who constantly lifts up Jesus, who lives an exemplary life, who gives practical counsel about the life of faith and seeks to bring about revival and reformation—preparing people for the second coming of Jesus as John the Baptist prepared them for His first coming. This person would not be a "super prophet," superior in any sense to other followers of Jesus, but would be a humble servant of God, who is multifaceted in his or her equipping ministry on behalf of the people of God at the time of the end.

One reason we can be confident that such a person, or persons, should come at the time of the end is that our Lord warned us against "false" prophets. Jesus said, "For false christs and false prophets will rise and show great signs and wonders to deceive, if possible, even the elect. See, I have told you beforehand" (Matthew 24:24, 25). The fact that Jesus warns us against false *prophets* in the last days suggests that there will be genuine prophets. If He didn't expect genuine prophets at the time of the end, He would have warned us about *any* prophets—not just false prophets. Instead, He warned about *false* prophets, wanting His church to know the difference between them and His true prophets.[5]

The testimony of Jesus

Revelation 12 reveals four stages in the great conflict between good and evil, between Christ and Satan. The first stage takes place in heaven, where the dragon, Satan, fights against

Michael and His angels, but does not succeed. He is eventually expelled and comes down to earth (see Revelation 12:7–12).

The second stage finds the dragon ready to pounce on the Child from the "woman," God's followers, or the church. This Child is a reference to Jesus, since He was "to rule all nations with a rod of iron" and was "caught up to God and His throne" (verse 5). Again, the devil failed in his objective.

In the third stage, the "woman" flees "into the wilderness"[6] for 1,260 days (years). Even though the dragon "spewed water out of his mouth like a flood" to drown God's followers, "the earth helped the woman, and the earth opened its mouth and swallowed up the flood," frustrating the devil's plans once more (verses 15, 16).

Note the sequence: First, Satan goes after God and is cast out of heaven. Next, he goes after the incarnate Christ, and Jesus is caught up to God. Then, he persecutes the "woman," the people of God, and she is delivered.

Finally, in the fourth stage, the dragon, "enraged with the woman," goes off "to make war with the rest of her offspring" (verse 17). But this time, we are not told the outcome—at least not yet. These "offspring" are the children of the "woman," God's people living at the time of the end. They are the remnant, the last group, before Christ returns in glory. They "keep the commandments of God and have the testimony of Jesus Christ" (verse 17). Their shield against the dragon is their identity as God's people. As long as they keep trusting what God commands and holding on to the testimony of Jesus, they will be safe.

What is the "testimony of Jesus"? In this case, the book of Revelation itself can help us. The angel said to John, "I am your fellow servant, and of your brethren who have the testimony of Jesus. Worship God! For the testimony of Jesus is the spirit of prophecy" (Revelation 19:10). So, the testimony of Jesus is the spirit of prophecy. And what is the spirit of prophecy? In Revelation 22:9, the angel tells John, "I am your fellow servant, and of your brethren the prophets." Since the "brethren" have the testimony of Jesus and since the "brethren" are prophets, *the testimony of Jesus is the testimony of the prophets, the spirit of prophecy.*

What does all of this mean? It means that God's last-day remnant church can expect to have someone who has the spirit of prophecy, or the gift of prophecy. It means that we can expect an equipping prophet to help the church be ready for the coming of Jesus.

God has never left "Himself without witness" (Acts 14:17). "Surely the Lord GOD does nothing, unless He reveals His secret to His servants the prophets" (Amos 3:7). He has done so in the past, and we can be assured that He will do so again. We can be sure that in His tender care for His end-time church and for the world at large, He will yet provide invitation and counsel through the testimony of Jesus, which is the testimony of His prophets.

Look for the fulfillment of that prophecy.

ENDNOTES

Chapter 1
Prophecy: A Matter of Life or Death

1. http://www.bookrags.com/research/david-koresh-and-the-branch-davidia-sjpc-03, accessed August 16, 2011. See also Harrison Rainie, "The Final Days of David Koresh," *U.S. News & World Report,* May 3, 1993, 24–31; Nancy Gibbs, " 'Oh, My God, They're Killing Themselves!' " *Time,* May 3, 1993, 26–41; Stuart A. Wright, *Armageddon in Waco: Critical Perspectives of the Branch Davidian Conflict* (Chicago: University of Chicago, 1995); and http://en.wikipedia.org/wiki/Timothy_McVeigh, accessed August 16, 2011.

2. About 27 percent of the Bible is predictive matter: 8,352 out of 31,124 verses in the Bible—28.5 percent from the Old Testament and 21.5 percent from the New Testament. See Gerhard Hasel, "Fulfillment of Prophecy," in *The Seventy Weeks, Leviticus, and the Nature of Prophecy,* ed. Frank B. Holbrook, Daniel and Revelation Committee Series (Washington, DC: Biblical Research Institute, 1986), 3:288, 296.

3. Everett F. Harrison, *Introduction to the New Testament,* rev. ed. (Grand Rapids, MI: Eerdmans, 1971), 462.

4. Gordon D. Fee and Douglas Stuart, *How to Read the Bible for All Its Worth,* 3rd ed. (Grand Rapids, MI: Zondervan, 2003), 129, 130.

Chapter 2
The Abomination and the Coming Signs

1. Josephus, *The Jewish War,* 2.539, in *Josephus: With An English*

Translation, eds. and trans. H. St. J. Thackeray, Ralph Marcus, and Louis H. Feldman, Loeb Classical Library (London: William Heinemann, 1956–1965), 2:531.

2. *Eusebius' Ecclesiastical History,* new ed., trans. C. F. Cruse (Peabody, MA: Hendrickson, 1998), 3.5.3.

3. Tertullian, *Apology,* 16, in Ante-Nicene Fathers, 3:31, as cited in C. Mervyn Maxwell, *God Cares: The Message of Revelation* (Boise, ID: Pacific Press®, 1985), 2:29.

4. Most modern Bible translations say "beginning of sorrows," but the original literally means "birth pangs," or contractions.

5. Some scholars have suggested that Matthew 24 is Jesus' comments on the book of Daniel. Daniel's long-range prophecies, with their predicted apostasy, persecution, judgment, and ultimate exoneration of the righteous, gave shape to His Olivet discourse. See Hans K. LaRondelle, *How to Understand End-Time Prophecies of the Bible* (Sarasota, FL: First Impressions, 1997), 34, 35.

6. Tertullian, *On Prescription Against Heretics,* 36, in Ante-Nicene Fathers, 3:260, as cited in Maxwell, 53.

Chapter 3
The Story of a Wrong Approach

1. Much of this time prophecy will be explained in coming chapters.

2. In Hebrew thought, a "time" referred to an entire year, while "times" would be double that, or two years, and "half a time" would be the equivalent of half a year. Since the Jews considered months to be thirty days long, this prophetic expression, then, would be a span of time equaling 1,260 days (forty-two months of thirty days each).

3. Cited in LeRoy Edwin Froom, *Prophetic Faith of Our Fathers: The Historical Development of Prophetic Interpretation* (Washington, DC: Review and Herald®, 1950), 1:246, 247.

4. Ibid., 1:248.

5. Ibid., 1:257.

6. Ibid., 1:238, 239.

7. John Wycliffe, *De Veritate Sacrae Scripturae,* ed. Rudolf Buddensieg

(London: Trubner, 1905–1907), 3:267, 268, cited in Froom, 2:55.

8. Scott H. Hendrix, *Luther and the Papacy: Stages in a Reformation Conflict* (Philadelphia: Fortress Press, 1981), 111.

9. John Calvin, *Institutes of the Christian Religion* (London: Wolf & Harrison, 1561), 410.

10. Froom, 3:52.

11. Marcus Dods and Alexander Whyte, eds., *The Westminster Confession of Faith* (Edinburgh, Scotland: T & T Clark, 1881), 145.

12. See Roland H. Bainton, *Christianity* (Boston: Houghton Mifflin, 1964), 277–279. The Society of Jesus—the Jesuits—were the most influential development of the Counter-Reformation; see Kenneth Scott Latourette, *A History of Christianity* (New York: Harper Brothers, 1953), 850.

13. Some thoughts in this section I owe to Stephen A. Bohr, *Futurism's Incredible Journey* (Roseville, CA: Amazing Facts, 2009).

14. A basic principle of prophetic interpretation, already mentioned, is the day-for-a-year principle based on Ezekiel 6:4 and Numbers 14:34, in which a prophetic day represents a literal year. This principle will be developed more fully in chapter 6. However, a brief explanation is necessary here. Biblical writers considered months to be thirty days—never thirty-one or twenty-eight. So the forty-two prophetic months equal 1,260 prophetic days (forty-two months times thirty days each) or 1,260 literal years. The expression "time and times and half a time" (Daniel 7:25) is the equivalent to the same time span.

15. See Froom, 2:489, 490, for further details.

16. Bohr, 45.

17. *La Venida del Mesias en Gloria y Majestad* (London: R. Ackerman, Strand, 1826). The title in English is *The Coming of the Messiah in Glory and Majesty.*

18. For instance, it influenced Church of England clergyman Samuel Maitland (1792–1866), who then published a series of *Enquiries,* in which he vigorously argued against the Protestant application of the little horn and the beast to the papacy. His views ultimately influenced John Henry Newman (1801–1890), leader of what became known as the Oxford Tractarian Movement, a movement with the purpose of "de-protestantizing" the Church of England. Newman eventually became a Catholic.

19. *Dispensationalism in America: Its Rise and Development* (Richmond, VA: John Knox Press, 1958), 27.

20. *The New Scofield Study Bible* (New York: Oxford University, 1967), 3, footnote to the heading for Genesis 1:28.

Chapter 4
General Principles of Biblical Interpretation

1. See, for example, Winfried Vogel's "Why Do Christian Scholars Interpret Scripture in So Many Different Ways?" in *Interpreting Scripture,* ed. Gerhard Pfandl, Biblical Research Institute Studies, vol. 2 (Silver Spring, MD: Biblical Research Institute, 2010), 97–103.

2. For an insightful book on the many types symbolic of Christ's life and ministry, see Leslie Hardinge, *With Jesus in His Sanctuary* (Harrisburg, PA: American Christian Ministries, 1991).

3. Jesus taught two resurrections: one to everlasting life, the one referred to in 1 Thessalonians 4, and one to condemnation (see John 5:28, 29).

4. Herbert E. Douglass, *The End* (Mountain View, CA: Pacific Press®, 1979), 62.

Chapter 5
The Books of Daniel and Revelation

1. The meaning of these four beasts as stated is accepted with little variation by most scholars.

2. According to Kenneth A. Strand, " 'Victorious-Introduction' Scenes," in *Symposium on Revelation,* bk. 1, ed. Frank B. Holbrook, Daniel and Revelation Committee Series (Silver Spring, MD: Biblical Research Institute, 1992), 52, 53.

3. See introduction to the book of Daniel in *The Andrews Study Bible* (Berrien Springs, MI: Andrews University Press, 2010), 1107.

4. Justin Martyr lived in Ephesus, the same city in which John lived after his exile from Patmos, although Justin Martyr lived there a few decades later than John. He stated that "a certain man . . . whose name was

John, one of the apostles of Christ" was the writer of Revelation (*Dialogue with Trypho, a Jew,* 81, in Ante-Nicene Fathers 1:240). Irenaeus, a church leader in Gaul (France) at the end of the second century, knew Polycarp, who in his youth had known the apostle John. Irenaeus wrote that it was John who saw the "apocalytic vision . . . towards the end of Domitian's reign." *Against Heresies,* 4.20.11; 5.30.3; in Ante-Nicene Fathers 1:491, 558–560.

5. Maxwell, 2:63.

6. In addition to the "four big sevens," Revelation also contains seven blessings (Revelation 1:3; 14:3; 16:15; 19:9; 20:6; 22:7, 14); seven woes (Revelation 8:13; 9:12; 11:14; 12:12); seven spirits (Revelation 1:4; 3:1; 4:5; 5:6); seven lampstands or lamps of fire (Revelation 1:12, 13, 20; 2:1; 4:5); seven stars (Revelation 1:16, 20; 2:1; 3:1); seven horns (Revelation 5:6); seven eyes (Revelation 5:6); seven thunders (Revelation 10:3, 4); seven heads (Revelation 12:3; 13:1; 17:3, 7, 9); seven crowns (Revelation 12:3); seven angels (Revelation 8:2, 6; 15:1, 6–8; 16:1; 17:1; 21:9); seven golden bowls (Revelation 15:7; 17:1; 21:9); seven mountains (Revelation 17:9); and seven kings (Revelation 17:10).

7. Kenneth A. Strand maintains a complex eight-part chiastic structure. See his *Interpreting the Book of Revelation,* 2nd ed. (Naples, FL: Ann Arbor Publishers, 1982), 47–52. C. Mervyn Maxwell does this as well, however, with an important modification. See his book *God Cares: The Message of Revelation,* vol. 2 (Boise, ID: Pacific Press®, 1985), 54–62. Jon Paulien sees a seven-part chiasm in his book *Seven Keys: Unlocking the Secrets of Revelation* (Boise, ID: Pacific Press®, 2009), 39–43.

8. Strand developed these concepts more fully in "The Eight Basic Visions," in *Symposium on Revelation,* bk. 1, ed. Frank B. Holbrook, Daniel and Revelation Committee Series (Silver Spring, MD: Biblical Research Institute, 1992), 35–49.

Chapter 6
Principles for the Study of Apocalyptic Prophecy

1. See William H. Shea, "Unity of Daniel," in *Symposium on Daniel,* ed. Frank B. Holbrook, Daniel and Revelation Committee Series

(Washington, DC: Biblical Research Institute, 1986), 2:177, 178.

2. There is no historical or biblical evidence that this prophecy of Ezekiel 38 was ever fulfilled. We must look, then, at how the New Testament interprets this prophecy. Revelation 20 is the only place where reference is made to this text, where the terms *Gog* and *Magog* become symbolic of God's enemies at the end of time. Just as *Babylon* would become a code word for the apostate religious system in the last days, *Magog* is also symbolic. In this case, it appears to be a cipher, a language code. In Hebrew, the word *Babylon* is made up of only three consonants: *B, B,* and *L* (BaByLon). Likewise, in Hebrew, *Magog* is composed of the three consonants: *M, G,* and *G.* In the Hebrew alphabet, each of these three letters—*M, G,* and *G*—immediately follows the three consonants for Babylon—*G* follows *B,* and *M* follows *L.* Reversing the order of the consonants in Magog—*G, G, M*—solves the code. *G* stand for *B,* and *M* stands for *L.* Thus, *MGG* (Magog) is *BBL* (Babylon) reversed. See Jiri Moskala, "Who Are Gog and Magog in Prophecy?" in Pfandl, 237–239.

3. The explanation is offered in the next chapter.

4. In Hebrew time reckoning, one year was made up of twelve months of thirty days each; thus a total of 360 days. In this case, 2,300 divided by 360 equals 6 years and 5 months.

5. William H. Shea, *Selected Studies on Prophetic Interpretation,* Daniel and Revelation Committee Series (Washington, DC: Biblical Research Institute, 1982), 1:76.

6. The scope of this book does not allow us to explain each of these prophecies. The table is offered as a reference for readers who might want to study them.

7. Scholars agree that the Jews equated the expression "time" with one year, and "times" with two years. So, this is three and a half years of symbolic time. Multiplying 360 (the number of days in one year) by 3.5 years, results in 1,260 days or 1,260 literal years. Forty-two months (42 x 30) yields the same result—1,260 days or 1,260 literal years. These three prophetic expressions of time refer to the same span of literal time.

8. Unlike the previous prophecies of Daniel, this last vision does not deal with symbols representing the various kingdoms or powers, but with the historical kingdoms themselves, that is, until one comes to the King

of the North, which is symbolic. The last six verses of the chapter are understood by historicist scholars as yet to be fulfilled; see Shea, "Unity of Daniel," in *Symposium on Daniel,* 2:245.

9. This reference is among the most difficult to interpret within the most difficult apocalyptic chapter to decipher. For two views on the subject, see *The Andrews Study Bible* (Berrien Springs, MI: Andrews University Press, 2010), 1133, 1134, and Maxwell, 1:283–285.

10. Perhaps one of the best sources on the subject is Hans K. LaRondelle, *The Israel of God in Prophecy: Principles of Prophetic Interpretation* (Berrien Springs, MI: Andrews University Press, 1983).

11. This statement should not be construed as a "replacement" theology, the idea that the church has categorically "replaced" Israel. Neither is it "separation" theology, teaching that Israel and the church are two distinct entities. See Steve Wohlberg, *End Time Delusions: The Rapture, the Antichrist, Israel, and the End of the World* (Shippensburg, PA: Treasure House, 2004), 170.

12. For example, Hal Lindsay says, "Since the restoration of Israel as a nation in 1948, we have lived in the most significant period of prophetic history." *The Late Great Planet Earth* (Grand Rapids, MI: Zondervan, 1970), 51.

Chapter 7
Does Daniel 9 Teach About the antichrist and the Tribulation?

1. Carpathia appears as early as the third chapter in Tim LaHaye and Jerry B. Jenkins, *Left Behind: A Novel of Earth's Last Days* (Wheaton, IL: Tyndale House, 1995). The book in the series dedicated to this antichrist is *Nicolae: The Rise of Antichrist* (Wheaton, IL: Tyndale House, 1997).

2. When God told Moses to build the sanctuary in the wilderness, He instructed him to do it "according to all that I show you" (Exodus 25:9). This reference is picked up in the New Testament book of Hebrews, in which we're told that the Old Testament sanctuary and priestly ministry "serve [as] the copy and shadow of the heavenly things" (Hebrews 8:5). So, obviously, there is a sanctuary or temple in heaven, which doubles as

God's throne room. John the revelator saw it several times in his visions (see Revelation 4:1–5; 11:19; 14:17; 15:5; 16:17).

3. See the New International Version (NIV), the New American Standard Bible (NASB), the Revised Standard Version (RSV), the English Standard Version (ESV), and the New Living Translation (NLT), among others.

4. For a thorough examination of the validity of this date, see Arthur J. Ferch, "Commencement Date for the Seventy Week Prophecy," in *The Seventy Weeks, Leviticus, and the Nature of Prophecy,* ed. Frank B. Holbrook, Daniel and Revelation Committee Series (Washington DC: Biblical Research Institute, 1986), 3:64–74.

5. Cited in William H. Shea, "The Prophecy of Daniel 9:24–27," in *The Seventy Weeks, Leviticus, and the Nature of Prophecy,* ed. Frank B. Holbrook, Daniel and Revelation Committee Series (Washington DC: Biblical Research Institute, 1986), 3:95.

Chapter 8
Worship: The Big Issue in Revelation

1. Some thoughts are drawn from Franklin M. Segler and C. Randall Bradley, *Understanding, Preparing for, and Practicing Christian Worship,* 2nd ed. (Nashville, TN: Broadman & Holman, 1996), 6.

2. See W. E. Vine, *An Expository Dictionary of New Testament Words* (Old Tappan, NJ: H. Fleming Revell, 1966), s.v. "Proskuneo."

3. In the previous chapter, we saw how the 2,300-day prophecy would end in 1844. Evidently, the same applies to other prophecies such as the 1,290- and 1,335-day prophecies (see Daniel 12:11, 12), which are given in the context of the closing of the book of Daniel.

4. There is nothing in the New Testament to suggest that the seventh-day Sabbath has been done away with in the Christian dispensation. None of the eight New Testament verses referencing the first day of the week indicate worship (see Matthew 28:1; Mark 16:2, 9; Luke 24:1; John 20:1, 19; Acts 20:7, 8; 1 Corinthians 16:1, 2), even if most refer to the resurrection of Jesus. Neither Jesus (see Luke 4:16) nor His disciples articulated a need to change the day memorializing Creation (see Acts

Endnotes

13:42–44). Instead, they ratified the day based on the creation (see Hebrews 4:4, 9–11).

5. D. A. Carson, ed., *From Sabbath to Lord's Day: A Biblical, Historical, and Theological Investigation* (Grand Rapids, MI: Zondervan, 1982).

6. Sometimes people appeal to "first-day" texts in the New Testament as evidence that the Sabbath was changed for Christians. There are only eight such texts in the New Testament. Six of them (Matthew 28:1; Mark 16:2, 9; Luke 24:1; John 20:1, 19) simply refer to the resurrection of our Lord. Nothing is said in these texts about keeping the first day holy or worshiping the Lord on that day. In Acts 20:7, again, nothing there implies a change of day or practice. The church had gathered to "to break bread" and listen to Paul for the last time. Even if one considers that the breaking of bread implies Communion, there is nothing in the Bible that says that rite cannot be done on any day of the week. The last first-day text in the New Testament, 1 Corinthians 16:2, is simply an admonition to lay aside money on the first day of the week to help other needy churches, presumably before members would use all their money and couldn't help anymore. Nothing is said there about the first day of the week being holy or about worship.

7. See William H. Shea, *Daniel 7–12,* The Abundant Life Bible Amplifier, ed. George Knight (Boise, Idaho: Pacific Press®, 1996), 139.

8. Sigve K. Tonstad, *The Lost Meaning of the Seventh Day* (Berrien Springs, MI: Andrews University Press, 2009), 2.

9. Abraham J. Heschel, *The Sabbath: Its Meaning for Modern Man* (New York: Wolff, 1951), 29.

10. Paul Tillich, *Dynamics of Faith* (New York: Harper & Row, 1957), 41, cited in Tonstad, 9.

Chapter 9
Can We Expect Prophets at the Time of the End?

1. The Hebrew name *Methuselah* can be translated as "he dies" or "a sending forth." Some interpreters have combined both meanings into the phrase "when it comes, he will die." Although it seems a strange name to give to someone, Enoch, who was God's prophet (see Jude 14), named his

son *Methuselah* as a constant reminder that the Flood was coming. Many scholars agree that the year Methuselah died was the year of the Flood (see Genesis 7:11). This is perhaps one reason Methuselah was the longest living person ever—God kept him alive until the fullness of time for the Flood arrived. See Matthew Henry, *Commentary on the Whole Bible* (McLean, VA: MacDonald Publishing, 1706), 1:50.

2. Froom documents sixty-five Bible expositors on four continents between 1800 and 1844 who predicted the fulfillment of the 2,300-day prophecy to take place at some point between 1843 and 1847. See Froom, 4:403–406.

3. The scope of this book does not allow for the explanation of just how this prophecy was fulfilled in 1844. Readers are encouraged to attend the author's live prophecy lectures or study additional resources.

4. For example, Ahijah of Shiloh in the time of Jeroboam (see 1 Kings 14:1–17), Nathan in the time of David (see 2 Samuel 12:13, 14), and the daughters of Philip in the time of the apostles (see Acts 21:8, 9).

5. The Bible gives four tests whereby God's people may know if someone is a prophet of *God*. These are (1) agreement with Scripture (Isaiah 8:16); (2) Christian, or Christlike, fruit (Matthew 7:15–20); (3) recognition of Christ's human nature (1 John 4:1–3); and (4) accurate fulfillment of predictions (Jeremiah 28:9).

6. The previous reference to waters as representing people, nations, and multitudes (see Revelation 17:15) would lead us to conclude that the lack of water—the desert, or wilderness—represents unpopulated areas of the world.